STAR WARS

WORKBOOKS

4TH GRADE READING AND WRITING

FOR AGES 9–10

BY THE EDITORS OF BRAIN QUEST
CONSULTING EDITOR: BRYAN HOLLEY

WORKMAN PUBLISHING
NEW YORK

Library of Congress Cataloging-in-Publication Data is available.

ISBN: 978-0-7611-8939-8

Workbook series designer Raquel Jaramillo
Designers Tim Hall, Abby Dening, Claire Torres
Writers Bridget Heos, Megan Butler
Editors Nathalie Le Du, Megan Butler, Olivia Swomley, Zoe Maffitt
Production Editor Jessica Rozler
Production Manager Julie Primavera

Workman books are available at special discounts when purchased in bulk for premiums and sales promotions as well as for fund-raising or educational use. Special editions or book excerpts can also be created to specification. For details, contact the Special Sales Director at the address below, or send an email to specialmarkets@workman.com.

Workman Publishing Co., Inc.
225 Varick Street
New York, NY 10014-4381

workman.com
starwars.com
starwarsworkbooks.com

Printed in the United States of America

First printing December 2017

10 9 8 7 6 5 4 3 2

WORKBOOKS

This workbook belongs to:

_____

Who Is That Droid?

Who is used for a **subject**. Whom is used for an **object**. Whose is used for a **possessive**.

> **Who** is this pilot?   For **whom** is he working?   **Whose** astromech droid is this?

Fill in each blank with the correct word from the boxes.

| who | whom | whose |

His parents knew Luke Skywalker, _____ was Darth Vader's son.

He is friends with Princess Leia, _____ rebel army overthrew the Empire.

The pilot is clearly dangerous, but for _____ is he fighting?

_____ trained him as a pilot?

And _____ is the droid that is traveling with him?

Write a sentence using each word.

who
_____

_____

whom
_____

_____

whose
_____

_____

A Progressive Poem

Progressive verb tenses describe ongoing action.

> I **was watching** the sunset.   I **am watching** the sunset.
> I **will be watching** the sunset.

This poem is a tribute to Luke Skywalker. Underline the **progressive verb tenses**.

A Skywalker's Destiny

Yesterday, the suns were setting over the sand dunes,
And Luke was wondering when he'd fly away.
He was filled with sadness—stormtroopers had
killed his family.

The Empire is searching for him.
So he will flee his home planet with the rebel forces.
They will fight the Empire.
They will win.
It is destiny.

Complete each sentence using progressive verb tenses.

Luke was _____.

Leia is _____.

Han will be _____.

Collecting Adverbs

Where, **when**, and **why** are **relative adverbs**. While an adverb describes a verb, a **relative adverb phrase** describes a noun. **Where** describes a place, **when** describes a time, and **why** describes a reason.

This is the desert **where Rey lives**.

Fill in each blank with the correct relative adverb from the boxes.

where   when   why

Injustice is the reason _____ Poe fights the Empire.

Jakku is the planet _____ BB-8 meets Rey.

There was a time _____ Rey believed her family would return.

Finn remembers the day _____ Rey tried to convince him to join the Resistance.

Kylo Ren returned to Starkiller Base, _____ he spoke to Snoke.

Rey's Force-sensitivity is the reason _____ she heard the call of Luke's old lightsaber.

Write a sentence using each word.

where

_____

_____

when

_____

_____

why

_____

_____

Which or That

Which and **that** begin **describing phrases**. A phrase that begins with **which** can be left out of a sentence without changing the sentence's meaning. A phrase beginning with **that** *cannot* be left out of a sentence without changing the sentence's meaning.

> Wampas, **which** are carnivorous, live on the planet Hoth.
>
> Wampas **that** have caught prey hang it upside down.

Write a **C** next to the sentences that correctly use which or that. Write an **I** next to the incorrect sentences.

Creatures that eat only meat are called carnivores. ___

Creatures, which live on snowy planets, often have white fur. ___

Wampas, which are semi-intelligent, are dangerous to creatures and aliens alike. ___

Never travel alone in areas that are inhabited by wampas. ___

Creatures, which live on Hoth, must deal with freezing temperatures. ___

Stuffed wampas, which are furry but not ferocious, are popular children's toys. ___

Man Your Ships!

Read Dodonna's speech. Fill in each blank with the correct word from the boxes.

be	is	are

The battle station __is__ heavily shielded and carries a firepower greater than half the star fleet. Its defenses _____ designed around a direct large-scale assault. A small one-man fighter should _____ able to penetrate the outer defense. . . . The Empire doesn't consider a small one-man fighter to _____ any threat, or they'd have a tighter defense. An analysis of the plans provided by Princess Leia has demonstrated a weakness in the battle station. The approach will not _____ easy. You _____ required to maneuver straight down this trench and skim the surface to this point. The target area _____ only two meters wide. It's a small thermal exhaust port, right below the main port. The shaft leads directly to the reactor system. A precise hit will start a chain reaction that should destroy the station. Only a precise hit will set up a chain reaction. The shaft _____ ray-shielded, so you'll have to use proton torpedoes. Then man your ships!

AND MAY THE FORCE _____ WITH YOU!

One Beautiful Green Planet

When multiple **adjectives** are used in a sentence, they should be placed in a certain order, as shown below.

NUMBER/ DETERMINER	GENERAL OPINION	SPECIFIC OPINION	AGE	SHAPE	COLOR	ORIGIN	MATERIAL	+ NOUN
ONE	BEAUTIFUL				GREEN			PLANET
AN			OLD			FELUCIAN		SARLACC
A				ROUND			WOODEN	HUT
THE	DANGEROUS	OVERGROWN						FOREST

Place each set of **adjectives** in the correct order. Draw a picture to go with it.

Jedi interceptor
yellow   a new yellow Jedi interceptor
new
a _____

farm
humble   _____
the
Felucian   _____

days
long   _____
humid
two   _____

rancor
Dathomirian _____
one
ferocious _____

Luke's Lines

A **preposition** is a word that modifies a noun or pronoun to show direction, location, or time. For example:

at	after	before	into	on	across	in	with
behind	toward	to	beyond	under	until	next to	

A **prepositional phrase** consists of a preposition, noun or pronoun, and any adjectives or articles (**the**, **a**, or **an**) in between.

I stumbled **across a recording.**

Read each quote from Luke. Underline the prepositional phrase or phrases in each sentence.

I was going into Toshe Station to pick up some power converters.

Why are we still moving toward it?

I cut off my power, shut down the afterburners, and came in low on Deak's trail.

I won't be drafted into the Imperial Starfleet, that's for sure.

No, my father didn't fight in the wars. He was a navigator on a spice freighter.

It's too dangerous with all the Sand People around. We'll have to wait until morning.

The Empire won't bother with this rock.

I'll be at the Academy next season . . . after that, who knows.

Endor Under Attack

The Ewoks and Empire forces are fighting the Battle of Endor. Write a **prepositional phrase** to describe each battle pose.

This scout trooper is __on a speeder bike.__

This stormtrooper is _____

This Ewok is _____

This stormtrooper is _____

This Ewok is _____

In Too Deep

Read the story of C-3PO's experience. The words **too**, **to**, and **two**, and **there**, **they're**, and **their** are mixed up.

Circle the incorrect words.

Once again, C-3PO had the most terrible experience. Why, oh, why, do his friends love danger? Luke and Leia sent R2-D2 and C-3PO two Jabba's palace. They're plan was to trade the droids for Han Solo! Jabba refused too cooperate. Instead, he kept the droids as slaves. Imagine!

C-3PO became Jabba's translator. Jabba spent all his days listening too music and throwing temper tantrums. His friends laughed at his horrid jokes and cheered when others suffered. They were the most despicable people C-3PO had ever met.

Luckily, C-3PO knew his friends weren't going to stand by and let the droids suffer. Leia went to the palace disguised as a bounty hunter who had captured Chewbacca. That night, she snuck into Jabba's throne room and rescued Han. But Jabba discovered her plan and captured her—and Han, to! Oh, who would save C-3PO and R2-D2?

Luke arrived and tried to use a Jedi mind trick on Jabba so that he would set the droids free. It didn't work. Luke was thrown into a pit with a nasty rancor. He managed to kill the rancor, but his troubles didn't end they're. Jabba planned to feed Luke, Han, and Chewbacca two the Sarlacc. What could be a worse fate!

They all traveled across the Dune Sea to the Great Pit of Carkoon. Their, the heroes fought Jabba and his cronies. In the middle of the battle, R2-D2 revealed a secret. He'd been hiding Luke's lightsaber! With the powerful weapon, Luke turned the tables on Jabba. Luke and his friends defeated Jabba and his henchmen. Good riddance to bad rubbish!

Correct the circled mistakes.

Incorrect Word		Correct Word	Incorrect Word		Correct Word
_____	→	_____	_____	→	_____
_____	→	_____	_____	→	_____
_____	→	_____	_____	→	_____
_____	→	_____	_____	→	_____

Spelling Star

Write each of the spelling words two times.

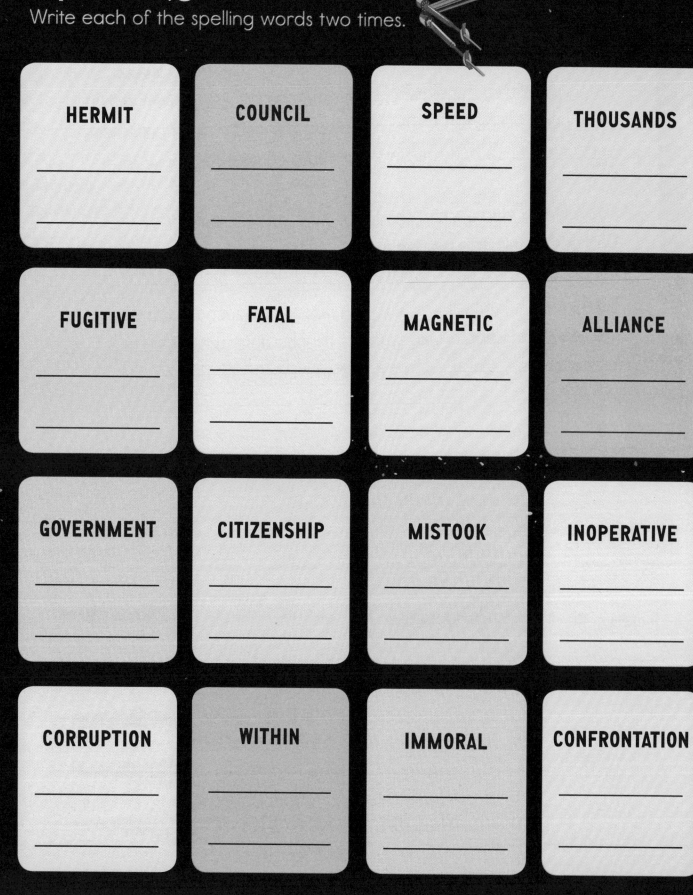

HERMIT
_____
_____

COUNCIL
_____
_____

SPEED
_____
_____

THOUSANDS
_____
_____

FUGITIVE
_____
_____

FATAL
_____
_____

MAGNETIC
_____
_____

ALLIANCE
_____
_____

GOVERNMENT
_____
_____

CITIZENSHIP
_____
_____

MISTOOK
_____
_____

INOPERATIVE
_____
_____

CORRUPTION
_____
_____

WITHIN
_____
_____

IMMORAL
_____
_____

CONFRONTATION
_____
_____

Choose any eight of the words. Write a sentence for each one.

_____

_____

_____

_____

_____

_____

_____

_____

_____

_____

_____

_____

_____

Punchy Punctuation

Quotation marks show that a character is speaking or being quoted in a text. **Commas** are used to punctuate a quotation.

> Kylo Ren said, "I had no idea we had the best pilot in the Resistance on board. Comfortable?"
>
> "Not really," said Poe.

Rewrite each sentence with the correct punctuation and capitalization.

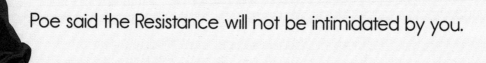

Poe said the Resistance will not be intimidated by you.

_____

Actually, the droid's not for sale stated Rey.

_____

Poe boasted I can fly anything.

_____

Poe explained I've got to get to my droid before the First Order does!

_____

_____

Finn insisted we need to get as far away from the First Order as we can!

_____

_____

Planets with a Capital P

Proper nouns describe specific people, things, and places—even planets. Proper nouns should always begin with a **capital letter**.

Obi-Wan Kenobi and Qui-Gon Jinn went into Lake Paonga to find the underwater city Otoh Gunga.

Read the facts about the planets. Draw three lines under letters that should be capitalized.

The capital city of naboo is theed.

A desert planet, tatooine is home to the dune sea.

On coruscant, the buildings are so high that air must be piped in so residents can breathe.

Battle droids are built on geonosis.

Jabba the hutt's palace is located on tatooine.

Anakin skywalker battled obi-wan kenobi on the edge of a lava lake on mustafar.

Princess leia was raised on alderaan.

Luke and C-3PO on Tatooine

When two or more characters are talking in a story, it's called **dialogue**. **Quotation marks** show that a character is talking. **Commas** are also used to separate the quotation and the story text. Each speaker's dialogue is in a separate paragraph.

Add the correct punctuation to the dialogue between Luke and C-3PO.

Luke, with his long laser rifle slung over his shoulder, stood before little R2-D2. "Hey, whoa!" said Luke. "Just where do you think you're going?"

The little droid whistled a feeble reply as C-3PO posed menacingly behind the little runaway.

"Master Luke here is your rightful owner   C-3PO said. "We'll have no more of this Obi-Wan Kenobi jibberish . . . and don't talk to me about your mission, either. You're fortunate he doesn't blast you into a million pieces right here

Well, come on. It's getting late " Luke said. "I only hope we can get back before Uncle Owen really blows up "

If you don't mind my saying so, sir, I think you should deactivate the little fugitive until you've gotten him back to your workshop,   C-3PO offered

Luke responded   No, he's not going to try anything."

Suddenly the little robot jumped to life with a mass of frantic whistles and screams.

"What's wrong with him now   Luke asked.

C-3PO answered   Oh my . . . sir, he says there are several creatures approaching from the southeast."

Luke swung his rifle into position and looked to the south.   Sand People!   he exclaimed. "Or worse! Come on, let's have a look.

A Dangerous Encounter

Imagine that Luke, C-3PO, and R2-D2 run into Tusken Raiders, also known as Sand People. Write dialogue for them. Be sure to use correct punctuation and capitalization.

_____

_____

_____

_____

_____

_____

_____

_____

_____

_____

                          _____

                          _____

                          _____

                          _____

                          _____

Dark and Light

Read the entries from the **dictionary** aloud.

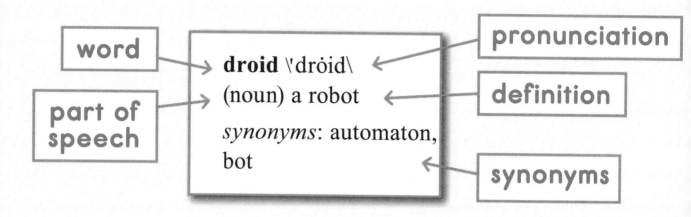

word		pronunciation
part of speech	**droid** \\'drȯid\\	definition
	(noun) a robot	
	synonyms: automaton, bot	synonyms

assured \\ə-'shu̇rd\\
(adjective) satisfied as to the truth of a matter
synonym: certain

charming \\'chär-miŋ\\
(adjective) polite in an interesting and friendly way
synonyms: appealing, delightful

clumsy \\'kləm-zē\\
(adjective) lacking ease of movement
synonyms: uncoordinated, accident prone

critical \\'kri-ti-kəl\\
(adjective) stating unfavorable opinions
synonyms: disapproving, judgmental

exceptional \\ik-'sep-shnəl, -shə-nᵊl\\
(adjective) unusual (often in a good way)
synonyms: extraordinary, remarkable

fatal \\'fā-tᵊl\\
(adjective) causing death
synonyms: catastrophic, incurable

A **synonym** is a word that means the same thing as another word. Write six sentences, each containing one of the synonyms from the dictionary.

_____

_____

_____

_____

_____

_____

An **antonym** is a word that means the opposite of another word. Using clues from the dictionary and the sentences below, replace each highlighted word with an antonym from the boxes.

charming   assured   fatal   exceptional   clumsy

Obi-Wan was surprised that Jar Jar got kicked out of his home city for being graceful.

_____

When they first met, Anakin thought Padmé was an angel, and she thought he was rude.

_____

Anakin's midi-chlorian count was normal.

_____

Qui-Gon Jinn was unsure in his decision to train Anakin to be a Jedi.

_____

When Obi-Wan saw that Anakin was on fire, he thought the flames would be healing.

_____

Kylo's Clues

Knowing the meanings of common Latin and Greek **roots**, **prefixes**, and **suffixes** can help you determine what a word means.

LATIN:

dict:	to say or tell
miss:	to send
spec:	to see, watch, or observe
trans:	across
vert:	to turn

GREEK:

demo:	people
gram:	written or drawn
graph:	to write
holo:	whole
morph:	change form or shape
poly:	many
tele:	distant

Match the words to their definitions by using the Latin and Greek roots, prefixes, and suffixes above.

dismiss

transgalactic

perspective

dictate

hologram

democracy

polymorphous

convert

telegraph

a whole, three-dimensional image formed by light beams

to say what must happen

a system of government in which the people vote for leaders and laws

crossing the galaxy

to send away

a point of view

a system for sending messages long distances

taking on many different forms

to turn someone or something into someone or something else

You Complete Me

A **complete sentence** has a subject and verb, and expresses a complete thought. An **incomplete sentence** or **fragment** lacks a subject or verb, or does not express a complete thought.

Write a **C** next to the complete sentences.
Write an **I** next to the incomplete sentences.

Anakin and Padmé married secretly. ___

When they traveled together to Naboo. ___

Because Jedi were not allowed to marry. ___

R2-D2 and C-3PO were the only guests at the wedding. ___

A spy told Emperor Palpatine about the wedding. ___

To tempt Anakin toward the dark side. ___

Rewrite the incomplete sentences so that they are complete.

_____

_____

_____

_____

_____

The Battle of Hoth

A **compound sentence** has two independent clauses joined by a **comma** and a **conjunction**.

Combine the independent clauses to form a compound sentence using a conjunction from the boxes.

so	and	but

Darth Vader sent an Imperial probe droid to Hoth __, and__ it found the Rebel Alliance's Echo Base.

Darth Vader planned a clever attack _____ his commander, Kendal Ozzel, carried out a foolish pre-battle strategy.

Ozzel tried to sneak up on the rebels _____ the rebels' defense sensors detected the enemy fleet.

The rebels were able to create a shield over the base _____ this prevented the Imperial fleet from attacking from the air.

Vader had to disable the shield _____ he ordered the AT-ATs to destroy the rebels' power generator.

Luke Skywalker tried to protect Echo Base's power generator _____ the AT-AT walkers managed to destroy it.

The rebels were forced to evacuate the base _____ the Galactic Empire won the battle.

The Empire thought the war was over _____ the rebels did not give up.

The Fetts

Underline the ten grammar, spelling, and punctuation mistakes in this story.

JANGO AND BOBA

Jango and boba Fett were like father and son. The family resemblance was greater than usual, because Boba was Jango's clone. As such, both were expert trackers and fierce fighters.

jango was born before the Invasion of Naboo Jango asserted that he was born on the Mandalorian planet Concord Dawn, but the Mandalorians claimed he had stolen his signature Mandalorian Armor, which he started wearing when he began working as an assassin and bounty hunter for hire. Jango became known threwout the galaxy for his skill in tracking down and fighting fugitives.

Because of this, count Dooku chose Jango to be the model for the clone soldiers he was creating. Fett agreed to provide his DNA for the clones and oversee their training. He was paid well, but he also asked for something else—one of the clones to raise as his son.

Jango tauhgt Boba the mandalorian ways. Boba loved and revered his father. Then tragedy struck. Jango sided with Count Dooku against the Jedi at the arena in geonosis and was forced to battle Mace Windu. Jango died as Boba looked on. Boba hated the Jedi for killing his father

Like his father, Boba grew up to be a bounty hunter, working for the likes of Jabba the Hutt and Darth Vader.

Jar Jar Jumble

A **run-on sentence** is a series of two or more independent clauses that are not separated by a conjunction, semicolon, or period.

> **Incorrect:**
>
> Jar Jar Binks caused a flood at an important party he was banished from Otoh Gunga.
>
> **Correct:**
>
> Jar Jar Binks caused a flood at an important party, so he was banished from Otoh Gunga.

Rewrite the run-on sentences as compound sentences by adding commas and conjunctions from the boxes.

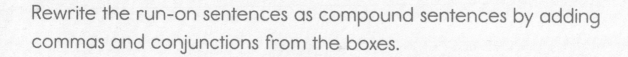

so   and   but

Qui-Gon, Obi-Wan, and Jar Jar traveled to Theed they rescued Queen Amidala there.

_____

_____

The four tried to fly to Coruscant their starship was damaged they landed on Tatooine.

_____

_____

They needed to fix the starship Anakin said he could earn money by podracing.

_____

_____

Anakin won the heroes left Tatooine.

_____

_____

Queen Amidala pleaded her case to the Senate they would not help Naboo gain independence.

_____

_____

Queen Amidala joined forces with the Gungan Grand Army Jar Jar became Bombad General.

_____

_____

Choose Your Words Wisely

Replace the crossed-out word with one of the more specific highlighted words below. Use the definitions and clues from the sentences to choose the best word.

Luke was ~~unhappy~~ _____ that his uncle wanted him to wait another year to join the Academy.

anguished: feeling extreme pain

devastated: having overwhelming shock and sadness

disappointed: feeling upset because something failed to meet one's expectations

Anakin Skywalker was ~~angry~~ _____ that the Tusken Raiders killed his mother.

incensed: extremely angry

miffed: slightly angry

sulky: pouting because of a bad mood

The pilot was ~~happy~~ _____ that R2-D2 fixed the starship's generator so they could safely pass the blockade.

contented: satisfied

elated: extremely happy

sunny: cheerful (used to describe a person's personality)

Han Solo ~~walked~~ _____ over to Princess Leia to joke with her.

sauntered: walked slowly without hurry or worry

strode: took long, quick steps

trudged: walked slowly due to exhaustion

Write eight sentences, each containing one of the highlighted words that was *not* used on the previous page.

_____

_____

_____

_____

_____

_____

_____

_____

_____

_____

_____

_____

_____

_____

_____

_____

Droid Disaster

Read the story of C-3PO's experience.

C-3PO just had a **horrid** adventure. It seems to happen to him a lot! This time, he was visited by his old friend Anakin Skywalker. As a boy, Anakin built C-3PO from spare parts. Anakin is all grown up now, however, and is a great Jedi instead of a slave. This made C-3PO swell with pride, until he realized that he may get swept up in Anakin's attempt to rescue Obi-Wan Kenobi.

To **accomplish** this dangerous mission, C-3PO and R2-D2 journeyed to the planet Geonosis with Anakin and Padmé. Once there, R2-D2 volunteered to help the humans. C-3PO worried that R2-D2 was too **obtuse** for this and had no sense of when he was needed or wanted. Well, R2-D2 didn't listen, and he followed Anakin and Padmé into the factory. C-3PO, a loyal friend, went too, only to be greeted by a distressing sight: droids making droids!

Before they knew it, R2-D2 **thrust** C-3PO onto the factory floor! That's when everything became **topsy-turvy**. C-3PO's head was attached to a battle droid's body! What a disaster! C-3PO was originally **programmed** to help, not hurt, so he was terribly embarrassed by his behavior on the battlefield. Attacking Jedi, name-calling, and firing a weapon—to what level would he stoop next?

All of a sudden, C-3PO's head went **soaring** off of his new body and onto the ground. Along came R2-D2, who dragged C-3PO's head over to his real body. C-3PO finally had a good head on his shoulders once again. In the end, R2-D2 was there to help his friend in trouble. Of course, R2-D2 was usually the one to start the trouble in the first place.

Context is the words or phrases that help define an unknown word's meaning. Context clues can appear within the same sentence as the unknown word, or they may be nearby in the passage.

important assignment
↓
"To accomplish this dangerous mission, C-3PO and R2-D2 journeyed to the planet..."
↑ ↑
(R2-D2 and C-3PO are   traveled
partners/teammates)

Based on the context in the story, what do you think the following words mean?

accomplish
- ☐ complete
- ☐ complain
- ☐ ignore

obtuse
- ☐ brave
- ☐ cautiously optimistic
- ☒ slow to understand

thrust
- ☐ pushed
- ☐ showed
- ☐ skipped

programmed
- ☐ destroyed
- ☐ designed
- ☐ brainwashed

topsy-turvy
- ☐ exhilarating
- ☐ upside-down or all mixed up
- ☐ swerving uncontrollably

soaring
- ☐ trickling
- ☐ flying
- ☐ jumping

horrid
- ☐ terrifying
- ☐ quick
- ☐ exciting

As Hungry As a Bear? What's a Bear?

A **simile** is a figure of speech that describes something by comparing it to something else. Adapt the Earthly similes to make sense in the galactic world.

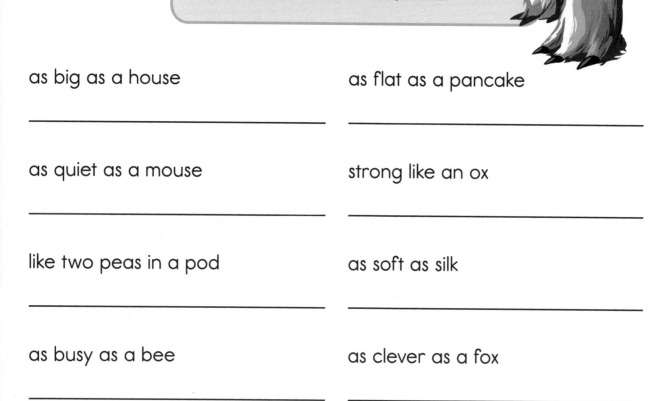

as hungry as a bear

as hungry as a wampa

as big as a house

_____

as quiet as a mouse

_____

like two peas in a pod

_____

as busy as a bee

_____

as flat as a pancake

_____

strong like an ox

_____

as soft as silk

_____

as clever as a fox

_____

Write your own simile by comparing your favorite Jedi to something.

_____

Write your own simile by comparing your favorite Sith Lord to something.

_____

Write sentences using each of your galactic **similes**.

_____

_____

_____

_____

_____

_____

_____

_____

_____

_____

_____

_____

_____

Galactic Proverbs

A **proverb** is a short, wise saying. Read each proverb and its meaning.

"Try not. Do, or do not. There is no try." —Yoda

Plan to succeed, and then put forth the time and energy required to do so.

A stitch in time saves nine.

Fixing something right away can prevent the need for more work later.

Two wrongs don't make a right.

Just because someone else behaves badly doesn't mean you should act the same way.

You can't have your Jogan fruit cake and eat it, too.

If you choose one option, the second option won't be possible.

Practice makes perfect.

To become good at something, you must practice.

Nothing ventured, nothing gained.

You can't succeed if you don't try.

You can't teach an old droid new tricks.

You can't change someone who is set in his or her ways.

Where there's smoke, there's fire.

When there are clear signs that something bad is happening, it probably is.

Write the **proverb** that offers the best advice in each situation.

When Qui-Gon Jinn battled a mysterious Sith, the Jedi wondered if the Order of the Sith Lords was making a comeback.

_____

R2-D2 wished C-3PO wouldn't be so cautious about everything. Didn't he get bored of doing the same things?

_____

Jabba the Hutt's rancor was hungry, and musicians were its favorite food. But Jabba didn't want the music to stop. What to do?

_____

Anakin was younger than most podracers. He wondered if he could really compete against them in the race.

_____

After Tusken Raiders, also known as Sand People, attacked Anakin's mother, he planned to hurt them in the same way.

_____

Luke said he would try to build a lightsaber.

_____

Luke was in a hurry and didn't have time to fix the landspeeder's rearview mirror. Later, he didn't see the Tusken Raiders approach. They tore off the rear bumper before he could escape. Now he had to fix that, too.

_____

On the *Millennium Falcon*, Luke trained with his new lightsaber against a remote. He was training hard, but felt that he still hadn't mastered it.

_____

The Skywalkers

A **first-person narrator** is a character who tells a story from her or his own point of view, using words like "I" and "we."

A **third-person narrator** is not in the story but tells the story, using words like "he," "she," and "they."

Read each passage. Circle the narration style.

Luke Skywalker grew up on a moisture farm with his uncle Owen and aunt Beru. By the time he was a teenager, Luke had seen many of his friends leave Tatooine to pursue exciting careers. For instance, Biggs Darklighter had joined the Imperial Academy, where he would learn to be a pilot. Luke begged Uncle Owen to let him go, too, but Owen said Luke was needed on the farm. Owen had another reason for wanting Luke to stay: He didn't want the boy to turn out like his father.

First person   **Third person**

I listen to all the traders and star pilots who come through here. I'm a pilot, you know, and someday I'm going to fly away from this place.

First person   **Third person**

My people, your people, all of our people—this war is meant to save them from suffering, not increase it. I support our brave soldiers, whether they come from the clone factories or from any of the thousands of systems loyal to the Republic, but if we continue to impoverish our people, it is not on the battlefield where Dooku will defeat us, but in our own homes.

First person   **Third person**

Though Princess Leia was only a baby when her mother passed away, the child remembered Padmé as kind but sad. Like her mother, Leia became a galactic leader. As Senator, she criticized Emperor Palpatine for his treatment of other worlds and helped build the Rebel Alliance. Leia also had inherited Anakin's gift of the Force—and his fiery temper. With these gifts, Leia led the Rebel Alliance in overthrowing the Empire.

First person   **Third person**

The Death Star

Read the story.

The Emperor, Darth Vader, and the Galactic Empire wanted to create the ultimate super-weapon to battle the Alliance. So, they created plans and began construction of the Death Star. The design was something that had never been seen before. It was a mobile battle space station the size and shape of a moon.

The plans for the Death Star included many weapons and features. From the outside, you could see a large circular dish that held a super-laser. On the inside, there was a command bridge. Here, Grand Moff Tarkin, who was in charge of the construction, presided over the battle station. His officers also worked there, overseeing viewscreens and the HoloNet. Around the outside of the Death Star, there were many docking ports for ships of all shapes and sizes. The docking ports were under the protection of powerful tractor beams. Inside of the battle station, there were thousands of military personnel, stormtroopers, droids, and starships. There were also the basics needed for them to live—sleeping quarters, restaurants, and even a hospital.

The Death Star was built in secret while orbiting Geonosis. This desert planet in the Outer Rim was the perfect secluded place to build a superweapon without being noticed. After many years of construction, the Death Star was moved to the orbit of the planet Scarif. This was an even more remote planet of the Outer Rim, where no one would notice the Death Star.

As the construction neared completion, the Alliance learned of the superweapon. The Rogue One team, led by Jyn Erso, set out to steal the plans for the Death Star. They succeeded! Princess Leia got ahold of the plans. She hid them inside of R2-D2 before she was captured by the Empire. R2-D2 was sent safely away in an escape pod.

Tarkin tried to get Leia to reveal the location of the rebel base by threatening her home planet, Alderaan. Leia gave the name of an old base, but Tarkin fired the Death Star's superlaser at the peaceful planet anyway. He wanted to make an example of those who oppose the Empire. Horrified, Leia watched as her home was destroyed.

The important plans inside R2-D2 made it back to the rebel base on Yavin. Using the information in the stolen plans, the rebels found a weakness in the Death Star. In the ensuing battle, Luke Skywalker fired a torpedo into a specific exhaust port. This blew up the Death Star's main reactor core and destroyed the entire battle station.

Use the story on the previous pages to answer the questions.

List five details about the Death Star.

_____

_____

_____

_____

_____

What details in the story show that it would be hard to destroy?

_____

_____

What do you think the rebels thought when they found out about the Death Star? Why? Refer to a specific detail in the story.

_____

_____

_____

_____

Finish writing the movie preview for this story. Tell people what the story is about and why they should see it.

In a world where the Empire and the Alliance wage ongoing battles, one superweapon may change everything . . .

_____

_____

_____

_____

_____

Draw a movie poster for this story. Include the title of the movie, a sentence about it, and an illustration based on the story. Underline the sentences in the story that gave you the details for the illustration.

What Happens Next?

Complete the story. Use **dialogue** and **description** to show how the characters respond to the situation.

> At the Niima Outpost on Jakku, Rey and BB-8 meet Finn. BB-8 points out some stormtroopers who are looking for them! Finn and Rey grab ahold of each other's hands and run, zigzagging through the tents. They take cover in a tent until Finn hears something alarming. He pulls Rey out of the tent, with BB-8 close behind. A TIE fighter appears and fires at them! The explosion sends them flying, but they are okay. Under attack, Finn yells, "We can't outrun them!"
>
> "We might in that quad jumper!" Rey screams, pointing at an old ship.
>
> They continue running from the stormtroopers ...

_____

_____

_____

_____

_____

_____

_____

_____

_____

The Legend of the Force

Read about the Force from two different points of view.

THE LIGHT SIDE

"A Jedi uses the Force for knowledge and defense, never for attack." —YODA

The Force exists in all of the galaxy as an energy field that connects living things. Master Yoda once said, "My ally is the Force, and a powerful ally it is. Life creates it, makes it grow. Its energy surrounds us and binds us."

Some are Force-sensitive. This means that they have a high level of midi-chlorians in their blood. Those that are Force-sensitive can use and harness the powers of the Force around them. They can often sense attacks before they happen, control and move objects with their minds, and even influence the thoughts of others. The Jedi are Force-sensitive.

The Jedi are those who have studied the Force and committed to using it only to help those in need. New Jedi are taught that the Force can be used for protection, wisdom, and much more. Over time, they have spread all over the galaxy, fighting for peace and justice. Obi-Wan Kenobi said it most clearly: "The Force is what gives a Jedi his power."

But beware—the Force has two sides: the light side and the dark side. Both are very powerful. Those who pursue the dark side use the Force to try to gain power for themselves. The dark side has only the power to destroy. The light side, on the other hand, has the power to build, to heal, and to defend. Always choose light. It is the way of the Jedi.

THE DARK SIDE

"From my point of view, the Jedi are evil." —ANAKIN SKYWALKER

The Jedi would have you believe that they have always chosen the light side of the Force. These members of the Jedi Order, the ones who felt that only the light side should be used, were weak. Rather than taking the power that was rightfully theirs and ruling the galaxy, they chose only to help those in need. Some Jedi couldn't stand by and watch the Order grow weak. So they formed a new collective called the Sith Order and fought against the Jedi.

The Sith were the true followers of the Force—they focused on anger, fear, and pain to gain power. They knew that you could actually accomplish much by using the dark side, because the dark side was far more powerful. It could be used to make Force lightning, defeat enemies, and even prevent death.

Anakin Skywalker was Force-sensitive. He had the highest midi-chlorian count ever recorded. He became a great and very powerful Jedi. Then, he turned to the dark side and became a Sith Lord. As a Sith Lord, known as Darth Vader, he became a great leader for the Empire.

Over time, the Jedi Order was destroyed. Any surviving Jedi went into hiding. The Jedi say they fight for good, but they refuse to take charge. Sith, on the other hand, use the dark side to gain power. And with that power, we can do good. Or bad. We can do whatever we want! Always choose the dark side. It's the way to true power.

Answer the questions.

From whose point of view is "The Light Side" on page 44 told?

_____

From whose point of view is "The Dark Side" on page 45 told?

_____

What do the light side and the dark side represent to the Jedi?

_____

What do the light side and the dark side represent to the Sith?

_____

Write two details that are alike in both stories.

_____

_____

Write two details that are not alike in the two stories.

_____

_____

_____

_____

Which of these arguments is NOT made in "The Light Side" on page 44?

a. The Force should be used to fight for justice, not power.
b. It is okay to use the dark side, but only to help others.
c. The dark side is powerful.

Draw a picture based on each story that shows the contrasting descriptions of "The Legend of the Force."

A Mos Eisley Meeting

A **play** is a piece of writing that is supposed to be performed by actors. The people in the play are the **cast of characters**. The **props** are items used by the characters. The **exposition** gives background information that the audience needs to understand the play. **Stage directions** describe the actions the characters will do. Read the following play aloud. Act out the different parts.

SETTING: A busy street in Mos Eisley, on Tatooine

CAST OF CHARACTERS: LUKE SKYWALKER, BEN KENOBI, R2-D2, C-3PO, AND A HANDFUL OF STORMTROOPERS

PROPS: LUKE'S ID CARD

EXPOSITION: Together, Luke, Ben Kenobi, and the two droids, R2-D2 and C-3PO, are headed to Mos Eisley. Ben is searching there for transport to Alderaan. At the same time, the Empire is searching for the missing rebel droids. Luke's speeder is stopped on the crowded street by a handful of stormtroopers. The stormtroopers look at the droids suspiciously and begin to question Luke.

STORMTROOPER: How long have you had these droids?

LUKE: About three or four seasons.

BEN KENOBI: They're for sale if you want them.

STORMTROOPER: Let me see your identification.

(Luke nervously searches to find his ID.)

BEN KENOBI: You don't need to see his identification.

STORMTROOPER: We don't need to see his identification.

BEN KENOBI: These are not the droids you're looking for.

STORMTROOPER: These are not the droids we're looking for.

BEN KENOBI: He can go about his business.

STORMTROOPER: You can go about your business.

BEN KENOBI: Move along.

STORMTROOPER: Move along. Move along.

(Luke drives the speeder off quickly and approaches a cantina.)

Write the next scene in "A Mos Eisley Meeting." Include stage directions in parentheses, if necessary.

Setting: _____

Cast of Characters: _____

Props: _____

_____

_____

_____

_____

_____

_____

_____

_____

_____

_____

_____

_____

_____

_____

An Ode for Anakin

A **verse** in a poem is a group of lines. Verses are separated by a blank line. **Rhyme scheme** is the way the words in a poem rhyme. Read the following poem about Anakin aloud.

Anakin's Fall

He was the Chosen One,
The pride of Qui-Gon.
How did he fall so far
From where he had begun?

They meet again on Mustafar.
Padmé tells the truth; Anakin calls her a liar.
Qui-Gon must protect Padmé from his rage.
Anakin is on the dark side of this war.

They fight beside the angry sea.
Who will be the one to go free?

Follow the directions.

Circle the first verse of the poem.

Circle whether the poem has a rhyme scheme or not.

Rhymes   Does not rhyme

Underline the theme of the poem.

True friendship can never die.

Anger can poison even the best of us.

Nobody is perfect.

Change is the only constant.

Rewrite the poem as a **play**. Include **dialogue** for both Obi-Wan and Anakin. Write any **stage directions**, or actions, in parentheses.

Setting: _____

Cast of Characters: _____

Props: _____

_____

_____

_____

_____

_____

_____

_____

_____

_____

_____

_____

_____

_____

Clone Troopers

Read the story.

Perfect Soldiers

Clone troopers are perfect soldiers, if "perfect" means carrying out orders without question. Before the Invasion of Naboo, Jedi Master Sifo-Dyas began to suspect that there were dark days ahead for the Republic and that it would need an army to protect itself. However, the Jedi Council rejected his ideas. So Sifo-Dyas secretly contacted the Kaminoans, who were experts in cloning. Together, they created an army of clone soldiers without the approval of the Jedi Council or Galactic Senate.

Soon after, Sifo-Dyas was killed by a Sith, who took over the operation of creating the clone army. The Sith used bounty hunter Jango Fett as the template for all the clones. The clones were given Fett's DNA so they would look like him and act like him. They would have his concentration, discipline, and athleticism. However, they would be slightly altered so that, unlike Fett, they wouldn't think for themselves. Instead, they were engineered to obey the Republic without question.

The troopers grew as babies in cloning chambers on Kamino. Then, from the earliest age, they were trained to fight—and obey. They learned to handle weapons, shoot, and work together as a team. At the end of their training, they were outfitted in protective uniforms, similar to what Jango Fett wore as a bounty hunter.

Though the clone troopers were originally created by a Jedi, the Jedi Council was not told about them. Obi-Wan only learned of the troopers by chance. He was investigating a bounty hunter who had tried to assassinate Senator Padmé Amidala and learned that one of his weapons came from the remote planet Kamino. When Obi-Wan traveled there, he was greeted with open arms. The Kaminoans had been waiting for a Jedi to arrive to claim the army. The discovery came at the perfect time. The Jedi had been fighting a Separatist movement and needed reinforcements. Now they had just that in the form of clone troopers—two hundred thousand of them.

On Kamino, Obi-Wan also found out that Padmé's would-be assassin, Zam Wesell, was hired by Jango Fett—the model for the clone troopers. When Obi-Wan chased Fett to Geonosis, the Jedi was captured by Count Dooku, a Jedi turned Sith Lord. Anakin and Padmé set out to rescue Obi-Wan but were captured themselves. Dooku unleashed his battle droids on the team. The situation seemed hopeless, until Yoda arrived with the clone troopers. The battle was won, but it was only the beginning.

As Yoda said, "Begun, the Clone War has." The war's name shows just how important the clones were to its endeavor. Led by Jedi generals, the clones fought the Separatist army bravely. Indeed, after a few years, the Republic was on the verge of winning the war. Then the clones' obedience took a tragic turn. They were ordered by Palpatine— Chancellor of the Republic and a secret Sith—to kill the Jedi generals. Palpatine turned the Republic into his own evil empire, which the clones would now serve without question.

A **main idea** tells what a story is about. **Supporting details** are facts, descriptions, and examples that help prove or illustrate the main idea.

Follow the directions.

Circle the main idea of this text.

Even though the clone troopers were similar to one another, the Jedi saw each as an individual.

Clone troopers were brave and capable, but also dangerous because they followed orders without question.

Palpatine betrayed the Empire when he ordered the Jedi to be killed.

Circle the supporting detail from the text that suggests that the Sith were behind the creation of the clone troopers all along.

The Kaminoans had been waiting for a Jedi to arrive to claim the army.

Led by their Jedi generals, the clones fought the Separatist army bravely.

Sifo-Dyas was killed by a Sith, who took over the operation of creating the clone army.

Why was it so dangerous for the clone troopers not to be able to think for themselves? Support your argument with details and examples from the text.

_____

_____

_____

_____

Why was Jango Fett used as a model for clone troopers? Support your argument with details and examples from the text.

_____

_____

If you were a Jedi who trained the clone troopers, what types of orders would you tell them to follow or not follow?

You should follow orders that _____.

You shouldn't follow orders that _____.

A **firsthand account** is based on the author's personal experience. Examples include a diary, autobiography, or personal blog post. A **secondhand account** is based on the author's research. It may include information from an article or history book.

Pretend you are a clone trooper. Write a firsthand account about your training as a soldier.

As a clone trooper, I _____

_____

_____

_____

_____

_____

_____

_____

_____

Compare your firsthand account with the secondhand account on pages 52–53.

What does your firsthand account have that the secondhand account does not?

_____

_____

What does the secondhand account have that your firsthand account does not?

_____

_____

The Queen's Starship

A **diagram** is a drawing that shows how something looks or works. Study the diagram and read the description. Then answer the questions.

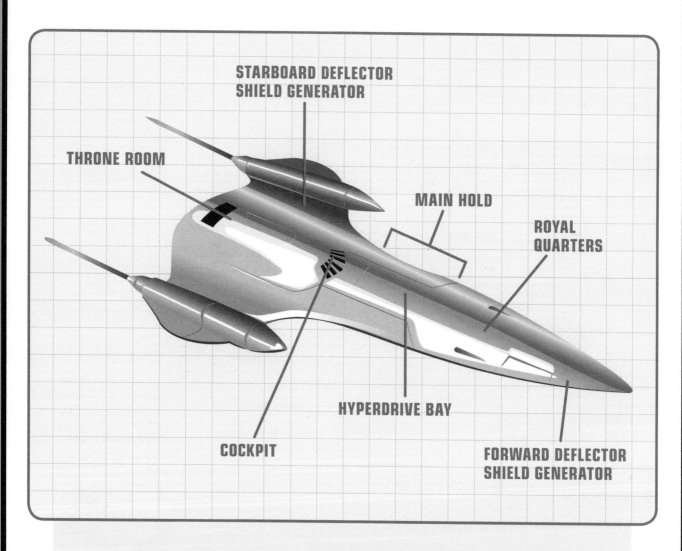

The queen of Naboo, Queen Amidala, had her own custom starship. It was called the Naboo Royal Starship. She used it to travel to royal affairs and interplanetary events. Inside, there were private quarters where she could sleep, and there was even a royal throne room. The starship also had a fast hyperdrive core and an escape pod for emergencies. You'll see from the diagram what the starship is missing: weapons. Because the people of Naboo favored a peaceful existence, even the queen's royal starship included no weapons. It did, however, have strong protective shields.

My Starship

Design your own starship. Draw a diagram and label the starship's features. Then write three sentences describing how your starship works.

News Story

Read the holo communication.

ATTACK ON SENATOR AMIDALA!

SENATOR PADMÉ AMIDALA was the victim of an assassination attempt last night. The attempt was thwarted by Jedi Obi-Wan Kenobi and Anakin Skywalker. The would-be killer was caught but died before she could share key information about who is targeting the Senator.

Amidala was sleeping in her apartment on Coruscant as Kenobi and Skywalker stood guard outside. They sensed danger and barged in to find poisonous kouhuns crawling toward the young Senator. The creatures had been transported by a droid.

As Skywalker killed the kouhuns, Kenobi dove out the window to capture the droid. It sped off, with Kenobi clinging to it as it wove through the upper levels of Coruscant traffic. Watching from afar, the assassin saw this and shot the droid down, causing Kenobi to lose his grip and plummet. Skywalker, who had been following Kenobi and the droid, swooped down to catch Kenobi.

Together, Kenobi and Skywalker chased the mysterious assassin, with Skywalker diving through the sky and onto her speeder. This led to the speeder crashing on the streets of Coruscant. Skywalker chased the assassin on foot until she disappeared inside a nightclub. Joined by Kenobi, Skywalker followed her into the club, where she attacked Kenobi. Kenobi disarmed her.

Before the assassin could reveal the name of her employer, she was shot by a poisonous dart. She did manage to reveal that her employer was a bounty hunter. The Jedi are now investigating the source of the dart. In the meantime, Amidala has been taken to a safe location and is under the protection of Skywalker.

Chronological order is the order in which events happen. Rewrite the article as a story in a comic book or graphic novel. Fill in the missing **panels** so that the action is in chronological order.

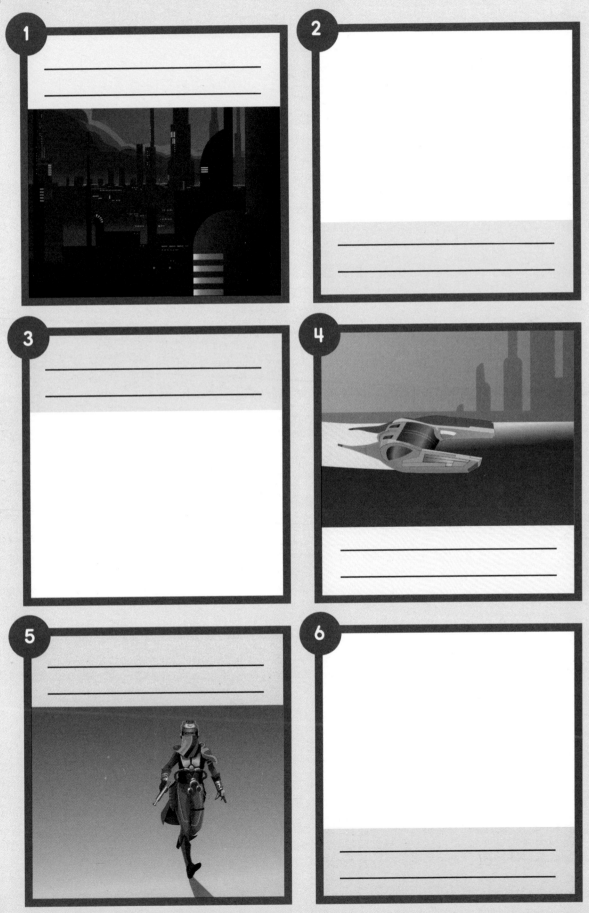

Worlds Apart

Read about the home planets.

Father and son, Anakin and Luke Skywalker were both raised on the desert planet Tatooine. With two suns, it was quite hot during the day. It was so remote that neither the Galactic Republic nor the Empire considered it to be under their domain. Instead, the Hutts—a crime family—ruled the planet. In spite of its remote location, it did have a few port cities, including Mos Espa, where Anakin and his mother, Shmi, were slaves to a junk dealer.

Had Anakin not fallen to the dark side, Luke and Leia likely would have been raised on Coruscant, where their mother served in the Senate and their father served on the Jedi Council. Instead, Leia was adopted by Bail Organa and Queen Breha of Alderaan, and Luke was taken as a baby to live on Tatooine. Though the planet was no less dry or remote than it had been when Anakin was a boy, Luke did enjoy a more comfortable childhood. His aunt and uncle were moisture farmers, using technology to collect water vapor from the air. Though it wasn't a luxurious lifestyle, Luke's family owned a relatively large house, land, and several droids who aided them in their work.

Mother and daughter, Padmé Amidala and Leia Organa grew up on different planets. Both green and lush, Naboo and Alderaan were similar to each other and very different from Tatooine. Padmé's native Naboo had a watery core where Gungans lived in bubble cities. The surface of the planet was also rich in water. The capital city of Theed was built alongside a river, and beautiful waterfalls cascaded down from the royal palace, where Padmé served as queen. Naboo and Alderaan both had picturesque countrysides where people farmed. Their cities were rich in culture and wisdom and were home to more than a few universities. They were the kind of planets you would never want to leave. However, Padmé and Leia were not content to enjoy the comforts of home. Instead, they became inspiring leaders and traveled far and wide to promote peace and justice.

Circle the correct answer to each question.

How is this text organized?

To show events in chronological order   To compare and contrast things

Which of the following is true, according to the text?

Tatooine, Naboo, and Alderaan are all very different from one another.

Tatooine and Naboo are similar, but Alderaan is different from both.

Tatooine is different from both Naboo and Alderaan, which are similar to each other.

Best Base Planet

An **opinion piece** is a text that expresses your beliefs about a topic. Pretend you are a leader in the Rebel Alliance. Write an opinion piece to your crew about why you believe the fleet must go to Tatooine, Naboo, or Alderaan. To support your opinion, include information about the landscape, weather, and opportunities to find new military bases.

I Love *Star Wars*

Fill in the blanks to complete each sentence.

I think the best *Star Wars* movie/TV show/ book/comic book is _____

because _____.

My favorite character is _____

because _____.

My favorite part is when _____

because _____.

It makes me think about _____

_____.

It makes me wish _____

_____.

Draw your favorite scene.

Circle one of the **opinions** below. Then write a paragraph stating why you agree or disagree. Support your point of view with **facts** and **reasons**.

Joining the dark side was Kylo Ren's destiny. He really didn't have a choice.

Lando should have told his friend Han Solo that he was walking into a trap.

With everything he accomplished, R2-D2 is the greatest hero in the *Star Wars* franchise.

Finn claims that he doesn't like danger, but he clearly does, because he is always following Poe into harm's way.

_____

_____

_____

_____

_____

_____

_____

Can I Have a Tauntaun, Please?

Read the information about each creature.

Adopt-a-Creature

SPECIES: **Tauntaun**   HOME PLANET: Hoth
DIET: Fungus, lichen, small animals like Hoth hogs and ice scrabblers

With its thick fur, this snow lizard is as snuggly as it is stinky. And it's extremely stinky! It is large and docile enough to carry you and your supplies and can survive the coldest weather. However, on icy planets like Hoth, it does need shelter at night.

SPECIES: **Rancor**   HOME PLANET: Dathomir
DIET: Creatures, aliens

Big and scaly, this reptomammal isn't right for everyone. With sharp teeth and claws, it eats anything—and anyone—that gets too close. But treated with patience, a rancor can be trained to be ridden. Even so, it remains a danger to all those in its path.

SPECIES: **Bantha**   HOME PLANET: Tatooine
DIET: Plants, roots

Banthas are friendly and very furry. With their large bodies, long, hairy tails, and spiral-shaped horns, they can really stand out in the desert! They are tall and strong and can carry heavy loads. They can even give you a ride! Banthas like to live in packs, so consider taking more than one as a pet.

SPECIES: **Reek**   HOME PLANET: Ylesia
DIET: Plants

It may sound easy to feed a pet like this, but don't be confused! While it is an herbivore, in captivity they are often fed only meat to make them angry. So stick with plants to keep your reek happy. One clue will be color—when it is full and satisfied it is usually gray, yellow, or brown. But if its skin turns red— watch out! It means it is hungry and angry.

Transition words show the relationship between two sentences. Write a letter to your family to ask for one of the creatures as a pet. Use the transition words in the boxes. In the first paragraph, write why this pet would make a good sidekick. In the second paragraph, write why you would be a responsible pet owner.

first   second   for instance   in order to

in addition   in conclusion

Dear _____ ,

_____

_____

_____

_____

_____

_____

_____

_____

_____

_____

_____

Crash-Landing on Endor

Finish the story. Include the **transition words** in the boxes to organize the sequence of events.

next

then

afterward

earlier

later

Leia awoke with a groan. Her head hurt, and she quickly looked around to figure out where she was. She noticed that her clothes were torn, and she was sore and bruised. She saw something move in the corner of her eye, and she sat up, alert. A strange little furry face with huge black eyes came into view!

The Ewok was startled and grabbed his long spear, holding it toward her. Then he poked her with the spear!

"Cut it out!" Leia yelled.

She stood up, and the Ewok backed away.

She said calmly, "I'm not going to hurt you."

She looked around, sighed, and sat down on a fallen log.

"Well, it looks like I'm stuck here," she said. She looked up at the Ewok and . . .

_____

_____

_____

_____

Anakin Skywalker

Read the two stories.

ANAKIN ON TATOOINE

Young Anakin Skywalker's unique skills were apparent even as a young boy. He was raised on the Outer Rim planet of Tatooine. He and his mother, Shmi, were slaves. Anakin grew up in the bustling spaceport city of Mos Espa, which was controlled by the Hutts. He and his mother lived in the slave quarters. Their small and simple hovel was one of many slave homes stacked together.

He worked for his master, Watto, in a scrap yard. There, he sold scrap and replacement parts for spaceships, droids, and more. It was Anakin's speciality to repair the salvage that came into the shop.

Anakin displayed many skills. He was a talented mechanic at the scrap yard. He even built his own protocol droid, C-3PO, out of scrap to help his mother. He also secretly built a podracer, which helped him to become a skilled pilot.

ANAKIN THE JEDI

Young Anakin's path to becoming a Jedi began when he helped Jedi Master Qui-Gon Jinn. Qui-Gon made an emergency landing on Tatooine. Anakin raced his podracer and helped him to win the parts he needed for repairs. At the same time, Qui-Gon won a bet and secured Anakin's freedom from slavery.

Qui-Gon could sense the Force in young Anakin. He also tested his blood and found the highest midi-chlorian count he had ever seen. He asked the Jedi Council if he could train Anakin as a Jedi. The Jedi Council sensed fear and anger in the young boy, which was not the way of the Jedi. They refused Qui-Gon's request. Qui-Gon still believed that Anakin was the Chosen One. He believed that he could fulfill a prophecy to restore order and balance to the galaxy.

Before Qui-Gon was killed in a battle against the enemy, he asked his Padawan Obi-Wan Kenobi to train and care for Anakin. Obi-Wan convinced the Jedi Council, and Anakin's Jedi training began. Anakin was very loyal to his Jedi teacher, and his skills grew quickly. He became a successful Padawan, strong in the ways of the Force.

Choose one of the following topics for a paragraph about Anakin Skywalker:

Anakin's life before he met Jedi Master Qui-Gon

Anakin's many skills

How Anakin became a Padawan

In your own words, write the four most important things you learned about this topic from the stories on the previous pages.

1. _____

_____

_____

_____

2. _____

_____

_____

_____

3 _____

_____

_____

_____

4. _____

_____

_____

_____

A **topic sentence** states the main idea of the paragraph.

Using your notes, write a five-sentence paragraph about Anakin. Include a topic sentence at the beginning of the paragraph. The next four sentences should provide **supporting details** and **facts**. Draw an illustration about your topic.

_____

_____

_____

_____

_____

_____

_____

_____

_____

_____

_____

_____

_____

_____

Endor: Full of Surprises

Read the travel guide.

GALACTIC GUIDES: YOU NEVER KNOW WHAT YOU'LL FIND ON ENDOR

BY RALDO MEEKS

The forest moon of Endor is no place for the casual traveler, but for the adventurous at heart, the moon is a dream come true. Located in a remote corner of the galaxy within the Outer Rim, the forest moon of Endor is a magical and unexpected place filled with curiosities.

When you arrive, take a look around the lush moon surface. You will see giant trees making up the dense forest and tall mountains in the distance. The ancient redwood trees that fill the woodlands tower quite high in the sky. Up above you may see one, or both, of the suns.

Keep your eyes peeled for the moon's many surprises! On your trip you may meet one of the natives, an Ewok. You could even come across an Ewok gathering at Bright Tree Village, where many of them live. These furry aliens are short, and they most often have black or brown fur. You may recognize them because of their large, shiny black eyes. Perhaps you can catch them in action! Watch out for their spears, slings, and even hang gliders.

They can be friendly, but not always at first.

While exploring, you may want to be alert for signs of the Empire. They have been known to visit the planet. Some visitors have even seen Imperial scout troopers patrolling on fast speeder bikes. You may come across their old bunker, where one time they controlled a shield generator for the former Death Star.

One day on Endor, and you will see why it has so many surprises. That is, if you survive to tell the tale! The unexpected findings on this moon have made those who live there, the Ewoks, the intelligent and brave creatures that they are today. Stay on their good side, however, and you'll find that they are quite hospitable. Even helpful! Happy travels, my friends.

Plan a story about two people who visit the forest moon of Endor.

Describe the setting—how things look, sound, smell, taste, and feel.

_____

_____

Name and describe your two main characters:

1. _____

2. _____

Why do your characters visit Endor?

_____

_____

What problem happens when they first arrive?

_____

_____

How do they try to solve that problem?

_____

_____

Does it work? Does it not work? What happens next?

_____

_____

_____

How does the story end? (Remember, the conclusion should follow from the past experiences and events.)

_____

_____

_____

Write On!

Write the story you planned on page 73. Include transition words as well as dialogue and descriptions.

_____

_____

_____

_____

_____

_____

_____

_____

_____

_____

_____

_____

_____

_____

_____

_____

_____

Draw an illustration to portray your story.

A Letter to the Academy

Brainstorming is thinking of possible ideas or solutions.

Imagine that you want to apply to the Jedi Training Academy.
Brainstorm three things to write about.

Personal experiences and qualities that would make you a good Jedi:

_____

_____

Schoolwork and extracurricular activities that show you would make a good Jedi:

_____

_____

Evidence that you are Force-sensitive but will not succumb to the dark side:

_____

_____

_____

Write a **formal** application letter to apply to the Jedi Training Academy.
Include the information you brainstormed.

Jedi Master Yaddle
Jedi Training Academy
Kamparas Jedi Training Center

Dear Jedi Master Yaddle:

I would like to be considered for Jedi training at your academy. It is said
that "a Jedi's training in the Force never ends," and I am ready to begin
that challenge. I believe I would make a good Jedi because _____

_____

_____

_____

_____

_____

_____

_____

_____

_____

_____

Skywalker Timeline

Read the timeline.

46 BBY — Padmé Amidala is born on Naboo.

41 BBY — Anakin Skywalker is born to Shmi Skywalker. They are brought to Tatooine as slaves.

33 BBY — Padmé is elected Queen Padmé Amidala.

32 BBY — Anakin and Padmé meet. Anakin wins a podrace, thus winning his own freedom. He travels to Coruscant with Qui-Gon Jinn and Padmé, his first step toward becoming a Jedi.

25 BBY — Padmé is elected Senator of Naboo.

22 BBY — Anakin is assigned to protect Padmé from an assassination attempt. The two hide out on Naboo. The two then secretly marry, violating the Jedi rule against marriage.

22–19 BBY — Anakin and Padmé fight together in the Clone Wars.

19 BBY — Afraid that his wife will die in childbirth and thinking that the dark side can save lives, Anakin becomes a Sith, Darth Vader. He is badly burned while fighting Obi-Wan Kenobi on Mustafar and is rebuilt as part robot.

Having lost her husband to the dark side, Padmé gives birth to Luke and Leia and dies of a broken heart.

The Galactic Empire, ruled by Emperor Palpatine, takes power.

19 BBY–0 BBY — Luke is raised on Tatooine by Anakin's stepbrother, Owen Lars, and his wife, Beru.

Leia is raised on Alderaan by Padmé's friends Bail and Breha Organa.

0 BBY — Obi-Wan Kenobi, Luke Skywalker, Han Solo, and Chewbacca join forces with Princess Leia Organa and the Rebel Alliance to destroy the Death Star in what becomes known as the **Battle of Yavin.** It is the first step toward defeating the Empire.

3 ABY — During a lightsaber battle, Darth Vader cuts off one of Luke's hands and also reveals to Luke that he is Vader's son.

4 ABY — Leia learns that she is Luke's sister. She and Han Solo fight in the Battle of Endor.

During the Battle of Endor, Emperor Palpatine tries to bring Luke over to the dark side. When Luke refuses, Palpatine attacks the Jedi. Darth Vader defends his son, killing Palpatine. In the process, Vader's suit is badly damaged. On the verge of death, he tells Luke that he has saved his father. In death, Anakin becomes one with the Force. The second Death Star is destroyed. The war is won.

BBY = Before the Battle of Yavin
ABY = After the Battle of Yavin

Name two other things that happen the year that Luke and Leia are born.

_____

_____

_____

Number these events in the correct order:

The first Death Star is destroyed. _____

Anakin Skywalker becomes a Sith. _____

Emperor Palpatine dies. _____

Princess Leia grows up on Alderaan. _____

Which year came first, 19 BBY or 46 BBY?

_____

Which year came first, 3 ABY or 4 ABY?

_____

How old were Leia and Luke during the Battle of Yavin?

_____

Take Note

Research involves studying nonfiction material to learn more about a topic. Writing **research questions and notes** can help you to **categorize and organize** the information you learn.

Imagine that you have discovered Sith research questions and notes about lightsabers.

What types of lightsabers are there?

— Jedi

— Sith

— single-bladed lightsaber

— double-bladed lightsaber

— crossguard lightsaber (one large and two small blades)

How are lightsabers used?

— As a weapon in combat

— To defend against attacks, such as deflecting blaster bolts, reflecting shots back toward an attacker, and absorbing Force lightning

— To cut through objects such as blast doors

What is the history of the lightsaber?

— No one knows when the first lightsaber was created.

— Lightsabers have been in use for thousands of years, but were rare.

— Jedis began using lightsabers more often during the Clone Wars.

Conduct your own **research** for a report. Choose from one of the following topics and reread the material on the given pages:

The Fetts (page 25)
The Skywalkers (pages 36–37)
Anakin Skywalker (pages 68–69)

Below, write three research questions for your topic. Answer the questions by taking notes on what you find out on the given pages. Be sure to write your notes in your own words.

Question 1: _____

Notes:

_____

_____

_____

Question 2: _____

Notes:

_____

_____

_____

Question 3: _____

Notes:

_____

_____

_____

Plan It!

The **body** is the main part of a report. It comes in between the **introduction** and **conclusion**. The body of this report will have three paragraphs. Each paragraph needs a **topic sentence**, which states the paragraph's main idea, and it is good to have three **supporting detail** sentences. Follow the example and directions to write an outline for the body of your report.

There are several types of lightsabers that you can make.

1. The most common design is the single-bladed lightsaber.

2. There is also a double-bladed lightsaber.

3. Finally, there is a crossguard lightsaber, which has one large blade and two small ones, forming a cross.

Write a creative title for your report.

_____

Write a topic sentence for the first paragraph in the body.
(It will be similar to your first research question.)

_____

_____

Use your notes to write three supporting detail sentences:

1. _____

2. _____

3. _____

Write a topic sentence for the second paragraph in the body.
(It will be similar to your second research question.)

_____

_____

Use your notes to write three supporting detail sentences.

1. _____

2. _____

3. _____

Write a topic sentence for the third paragraph in the body.
(It will be similar to your third research question.)

_____

_____

Use your notes to write three supporting detail sentences.

1. _____

2. _____

3. _____

Begin and End

An **introduction** grabs the reader's attention and says what the report is about. The **conclusion** sums up the report and leaves the reader with something to think about. Follow the example and directions to write an introduction and conclusion for your report.

> **Introduction:**
> The lightsaber is the weapon of heroes and legends. Force-wielders, such as the Jedi and the Sith, used different kinds of lightsabers.
>
> **Conclusion:**
> Lightsabers have a variety of forms and uses, but they are especially helpful in combat.

Introduction (Write one sentence that grabs the reader's attention and one sentence that tells what the report is about.)

_____

_____

_____

_____

Conclusion (Write one sentence that sums up the report and one sentence that leaves the reader with something to think about.)

_____

_____

_____

_____

Draft It!

Use your outline to write a rough draft of your
report on this page and the next. Sketch two visual
aids in the boxes. These can be diagrams, maps, etc.

Editor Droid

Pretend that you are an editor droid. Read your research paper aloud and check for mistakes.

∧ Add text	⊙ Add a period	? Add a question mark
≡ Capitalize letter	ℛ Delete	◯ Spelling error

Grammar Checklist

☐ **Are my sentences complete? Underline any incomplete sentences.**
Because Yoda thought Luke was too much like Anakin.

☐ **Do my sentences end with a period, question mark, or exclamation point? If not, add them now.**
Luke could use the Force⊙

☐ **Are all the words spelled correctly? Circle any misspelled words.**
Padmé was elected (Senater.)

☐ **Are the letters capitalized at the beginning of each sentence and for each proper noun? Underline three times any letters that need to be capitalized.**
Padmé grew up on naboo.
                    ≡

☐ **Do my possessive words (Anakin's, Palpatine's, Padmé's) have apostrophes? Add any missing apostrophes.**
Anakin's mother waved good-bye.
       ∧

☐ **Have I used commas correctly? Add any needed commas.**
Anakin went with Qui-Gon, Obi-Wan, and Padmé.
                          ∧   ∧

☐ **Did I include transition words such as *first, second, in conclusion, in addition*, and *however* to show how sentences are related? Add any needed transition words.**
                                              however, he
Finn started out as a stormtrooper in the First Order. He followed his conscience
                                              ∧   ∧
and eventually fought Kylo Ren and the First Order.

Create It!

A **final draft** is the last draft of a report. It will be shared with others and should be organized, clear, and free of mistakes. Write a final draft of your report. Include the title, your name, and two visual aids in the boxes provided.

_____

_____

_____

_____

_____

_____

_____

_____

_____

_____

_____

_____

_____

_____

_____

_____

_____

_____

_____

_____

_____

_____

_____

_____

_____

Pretend you are making a holorecording of your report for a library in the New Republic. Read your finished report aloud.

Answers

pages 4–5

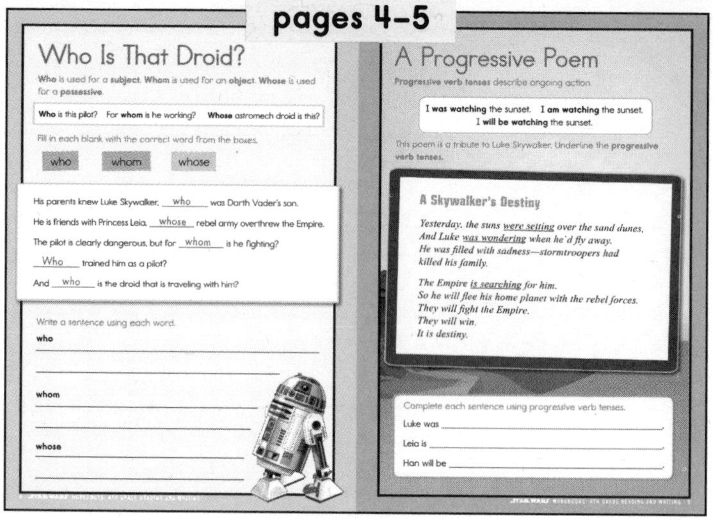
Who Is That Droid?

Who is used for a **subject**. **Whom** is used for an **object**. **Whose** is used for a **possessive**.

Who is this pilot? For **whom** is he working? **Whose** astromech droid is this?

Fill in each blank with the correct word from the boxes.

who whom whose

His parents knew Luke Skywalker. who was Darth Vader's son.

He is friends with Princess Leia, whose rebel army overthrew the Empire.

The pilot is clearly dangerous, but for whom is he fighting?

Who trained him as a pilot?

And who is the droid that is traveling with him?

Write a sentence using each word.

who

whom

whose

A Progressive Poem

Progressive verb tenses describe ongoing action.

I was watching the sunset. **I am watching** the sunset. **I will be watching** the sunset.

This poem is a tribute to Luke Skywalker. Underline the **progressive verb tenses**.

A Skywalker's Destiny

Yesterday, the suns were setting over the sand dunes,
And Luke was wondering when he'd fly away.
He was filled with sadness—stormtroopers had killed his family.

The Empire is searching for him.
So he will flee his home planet with the rebel forces.
They will fight the Empire.
They will win.
It is destiny.

Complete each sentence using progressive verb tenses.

Luke was

Leia is

Han will be

pages 6–7

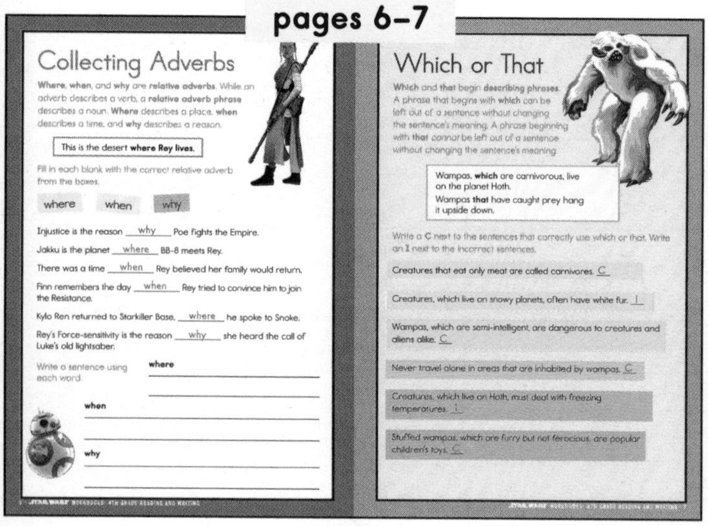
Collecting Adverbs

Where, **when**, and **why** are **relative adverbs**. While an adverb describes a verb, a **relative adverb phrase** describes a noun. **Where** describes a place, **when** describes a time, and **why** describes a reason.

This is the desert **where Rey lives**.

Fill in each blank with the correct relative adverb from the boxes.

where when why

Injustice is the reason why Poe fights the Empire.

Jakku is the planet where BB-8 meets Rey.

There was a time when Rey believed her family would return.

Finn remembers the day when Rey tried to convince him to join the Resistance.

Kylo Ren returned to Starkiller Base, where he spoke to Snoke.

Rey's Force-sensitivity is the reason why she heard the call of Luke's old lightsaber.

Write a sentence using each word.

where

when

why

Which or That

Which and **that** begin **describing phrases**. A phrase that begins with **which** can be left out of a sentence without changing the sentence's meaning. A phrase beginning with **that** cannot be left out of a sentence without changing the sentence's meaning.

Wampas, **which** are carnivorous, live on the planet Hoth.
Wampas **that** have caught prey hang it upside down.

Write a **C** next to the sentences that correctly use which or that. Write an **I** next to the incorrect sentences.

Creatures that eat only meat are called carnivores. C

Creatures, which live on snowy planets, often have white fur. I

Wampas, which are semi-intelligent, are dangerous to creatures and aliens alike. C

Never travel alone in areas that are inhabited by wampas. C

Creatures, which live on Hoth, must deal with freezing temperatures. I

Stuffed wampas, which are furry but not ferocious, are popular children's toys. C

pages 8–9

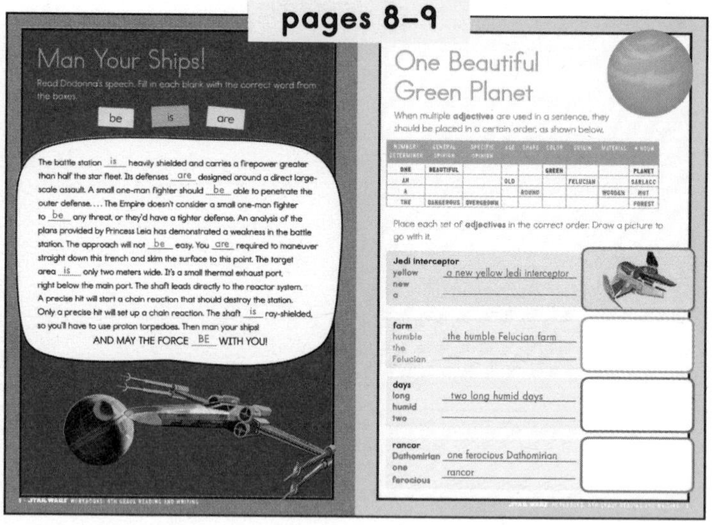
Man Your Ships!

Read Dodonna's speech. Fill in each blank with the correct word from the boxes.

be is are

The battle station is heavily shielded and carries a firepower greater than half the star fleet. Its defenses are designed around a direct large-scale assault. A small one-man fighter should be able to penetrate the outer defense. . . . The Empire doesn't consider a small one-man fighter to be any threat, or they'd have a tighter defense. An analysis of the plans provided by Princess Leia has demonstrated a weakness in the battle station. The approach will not be easy. You are required to maneuver straight down this trench and skim the surface to this point. The target area is only two meters wide. It's a small thermal exhaust port, right below the main port. The shaft leads directly to the reactor system. A precise hit will start a chain reaction that should destroy the station. Only a precise hit will set up a chain reaction. The shaft is ray-shielded, so you'll have to use proton torpedoes. Then man your ships!

AND MAY THE FORCE BE WITH YOU!

One Beautiful Green Planet

When multiple **adjectives** are used in a sentence, they should be placed in a certain order, as shown below.

NUMBER/ DETERMINER	GENERAL OPINION	SPECIFIC OPINION	AGE	SHAPE	COLOR	ORIGIN	MATERIAL	NOUN
ONE	BEAUTIFUL				GREEN			PLANET
AN			OLD			FELUCIAN		SARLACC
A				ROUND			WOODEN	HUT
THE	DANGEROUS	OVERGROWN						FOREST

Place each set of **adjectives** in the correct order. Draw a picture to go with it.

Jedi interceptor, yellow, new, a — a new yellow Jedi interceptor

farm, humble, the, Felucian — the humble Felucian farm

days, long, humid, two — two long humid days

rancor, Dathomirian, one, ferocious — one ferocious Dathomirian rancor

pages 10–11

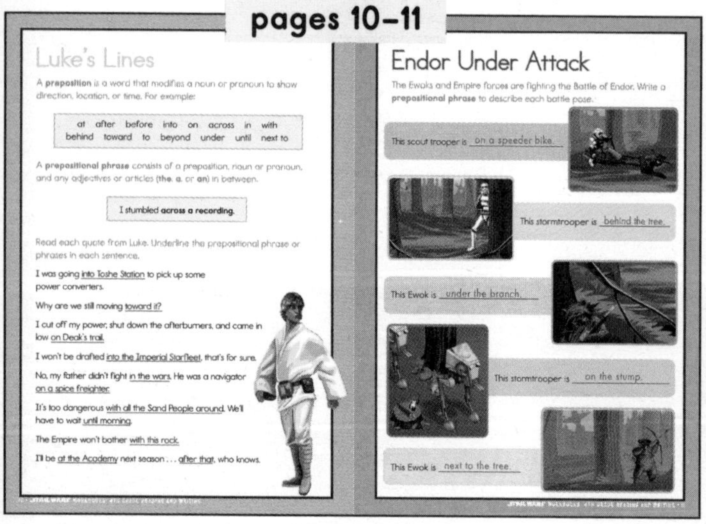
Luke's Lines

A **preposition** is a word that modifies a noun or pronoun to show direction, location, or time. For example:

at after before into on across in with behind toward to beyond under until next to

A **prepositional phrase** consists of a preposition, noun or pronoun, and any adjectives or articles (**the**, **a**, or **an**) in between.

I stumbled **across a recording**.

Read each quote from Luke. Underline the prepositional phrase or phrases in each sentence.

I was going into Tosche Station to pick up some power converters.

Why are we still moving toward it?

I cut off my power, shut down the afterburners, and came in low on Deak's trail.

I won't be drafted into the Imperial Starfleet, that's for sure.

No, my father didn't fight in the wars. He was a navigator on a spice freighter.

It's too dangerous with all the Sand People around. We'll have to wait until morning.

The Empire won't bother with this rock.

I'll be at the Academy next season . . . after that, who knows.

Endor Under Attack

The Ewoks and Empire forces are fighting the Battle of Endor. Write a **prepositional phrase** to describe each battle pose.

This scout trooper is on a speeder bike.

This stormtrooper is behind the tree.

This Ewok is under the branch.

This stormtrooper is on the stump.

This Ewok is next to the tree.

pages 12–13

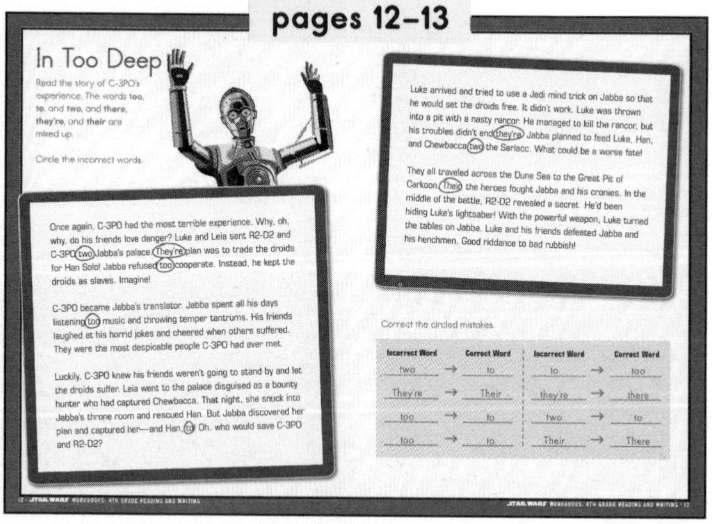
In Too Deep

Read the story of C-3PO's experience. The words **too**, **to**, and **two**, and **there**, **they're**, and **their** are mixed up.

Circle the incorrect words.

Once again, C-3PO had the most terrible experience. Why, oh, why, do his friends love danger? Luke and Leia sent R2-D2 and C-3PO two Jabba's palace. They're plan was to trade the droids for Han Solo! Jabba refused too cooperate. Instead, he kept the droids as slaves. Imagine!

C-3PO became Jabba's translator. Jabba spent all his days listening too music and throwing temper tantrums. His friends laughed at his horrid jokes and cheered when others suffered. They were the most despicable people C-3PO had ever met.

Luckily, C-3PO knew his friends weren't going to stand by and let the droids suffer. Leia went to the palace disguised as a bounty hunter who had captured Chewbacca. That night, she snuck into Jabba's throne room and rescued Han. But Jabba discovered her plan and captured her—and Han, too. Oh, who would save C-3PO and R2-D2?

Luke arrived and tried to use a Jedi mind trick on Jabba so that he would set the droids free. It didn't work. Luke was thrown into a pit with a nasty rancor. He managed to kill the rancor, but his troubles didn't end there. Jabba planned to feed Luke, Han, and Chewbacca two the Sarlacc. What could be a worse fate!

They all traveled across the Dune Sea to the Great Pit of Carkoon. Their the heroes fought Jabba and his cronies. In the middle of the battle, R2-D2 revealed a secret. He'd been hiding Luke's lightsaber! With the powerful weapon, Luke turned the tables on Jabba. Luke and his friends defeated Jabba and his henchmen. Good riddance to bad rubbish!

Correct the circled mistakes.

Incorrect Word		Correct Word	Incorrect Word		Correct Word
two	→	to	to	→	too
They're	→	Their	they're	→	there
too	→	to	two	→	to
too	→	to	Their	→	There

pages 16–17

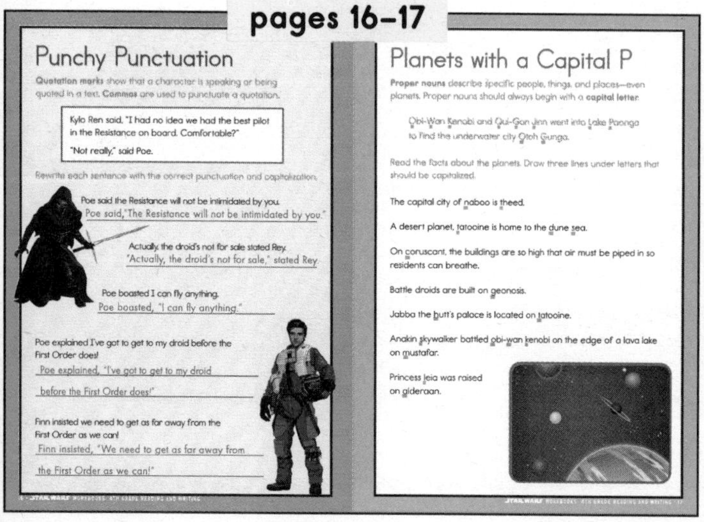
Punchy Punctuation

Quotation marks show that a character is speaking or being quoted in a text. **Commas** are used to punctuate a quotation.

Kylo Ren said, "I had no idea we had the best pilot in the Resistance on board. Comfortable?"
"Not really," said Poe.

Rewrite each sentence with the correct punctuation and capitalization.

Poe said the Resistance will not be intimidated by you.
Poe said, "The Resistance will not be intimidated by you."

Actually, the droid's not for sale stated Rey.
"Actually, the droid's not for sale," stated Rey.

Poe boasted I can fly anything.
Poe boasted, "I can fly anything."

Poe explained I've got to get to my droid before the First Order does!
Poe explained, "I've got to get to my droid before the First Order does!"

Finn insisted we need to get as far away from the First Order as we can!
Finn insisted, "We need to get as far away from the First Order as we can!"

Planets with a Capital P

Proper nouns describe specific people, things, and places—even planets. Proper nouns should always begin with a **capital letter**.

Obi-Wan Kenobi and Qui-Gon Jinn went into Lake Paonga to find the underwater city Otoh Gunga.

Read the facts about the planets. Draw three lines under letters that should be capitalized.

The capital city of naboo is theed.

A desert planet, tatooine is home to the dune sea.

On coruscant, the buildings are so high that air must be piped in so residents can breathe.

Battle droids are built on geonosis.

Jabba the hutt's palace is located on tatooine.

Anakin skywalker battled obi-wan kenobi on the edge of a lava lake on mustafar.

Princess leia was raised on alderaan.

pages 18–19

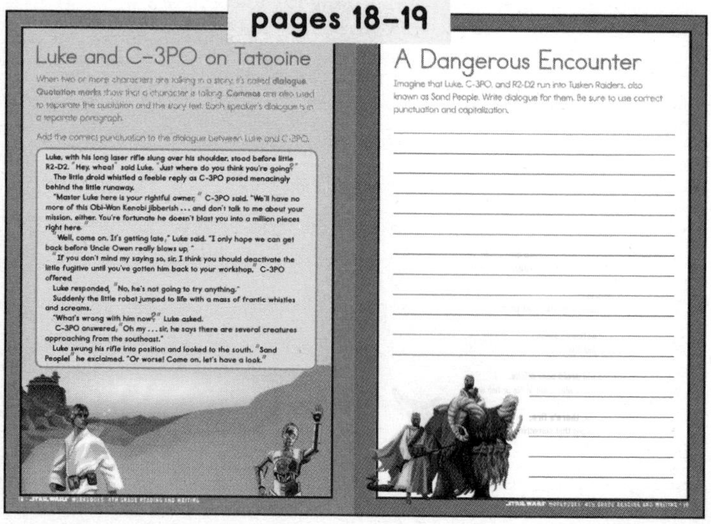
Luke and C-3PO on Tatooine

When two or more characters are talking in a story, it's called **dialogue**. **Quotation marks** show that a character is talking. **Commas** are also used to separate the quotation and the story text. Each speaker's dialogue is in a separate paragraph.

Add the correct punctuation to the dialogue between Luke and C-3PO.

Luke, with his long laser rifle slung over his shoulder, stood before little R2-D2. "Hey, whoa!" said Luke. "Just where do you think you're going?"
The little droid whistled a feeble reply as C-3PO posed menacingly behind the little runaway.
"Master Luke here is your rightful owner," C-3PO said. "We'll have no more of this Obi-Wan Kenobi jibberish . . . and don't talk to me about your mission, either. You're fortunate he doesn't blast you into a million pieces right here."
"Well, come on. It's getting late," Luke said. "I only hope we can get back before Uncle Owen really blows up."
"If you don't mind my saying so, sir, I think you should deactivate the little fugitive until you've gotten him back to your workshop," C-3PO offered.
Luke responded, "No, he's not going to try anything."
Suddenly the little robot jumped to life with a mass of frantic whistles and screams.
"What's wrong with him now?" Luke asked.
C-3PO answered, "Oh my . . . sir, he says there are several creatures approaching from the southeast."
Luke swung his rifle into position and looked to the south. "Sand People!" he exclaimed. "Or worse! Come on, let's have a look."

A Dangerous Encounter

Imagine that Luke, C-3PO, and R2-D2 run into Tusken Raiders, also known as Sand People. Write dialogue for them. Be sure to use correct punctuation and capitalization.

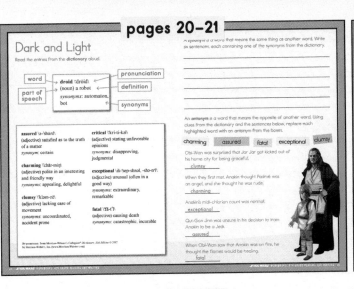

pages 20–21

Dark and Light

Read the entries from the dictionary aloud.

word → droid \'drȯid\
part of speech → (noun) a robot
synonyms: automaton, bot → pronunciation, definition, synonyms

assured \ə-'shu̇rd\
(adjective) satisfied as to the truth of a matter
synonym: certain

charming \'chär-miŋ\
(adjective) polite in an interesting and friendly way
synonyms: appealing, delightful

clumsy \'kləm-zē\
(adjective) lacking ease of movement
synonym: uncoordinated, accident prone

fatal \'fā-t'l\
(adjective) causing death
synonyms: catastrophic, incurable

critical \'kri-ti-kəl\
(adjective) stating unfavorable opinions
synonyms: disapproving, judgmental

exceptional \ik-'sep-shnəl, -shə-n'l\
(adjective) unusual (often in a good way)
synonyms: extraordinary, remarkable

A synonym is a word that means the same thing as another word. Write six sentences, each containing one of the synonyms from the dictionary.

An antonym is a word that means the opposite of another word. Using clues from the dictionary and the sentences below, replace each highlighted word with an antonym from the boxes.

charming · assured · fatal · exceptional · clumsy

Obi-Wan was surprised that Jar Jar got kicked out of his home city for being graceful.
clumsy

When they first met, Anakin thought Padmé was an angel, and he thought he was rude.
charming

Anakin's midi-chlorian count was normal.
exceptional

Qui-Gon Jinn was unsure in his decision to train Anakin to be a Jedi.
assured

When Obi-Wan saw that Anakin was on fire, he thought the flames would be healing.
fatal

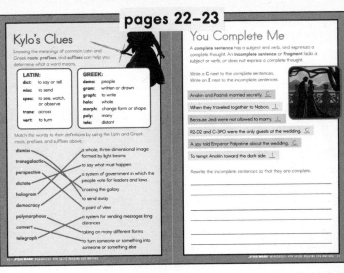

pages 22–23

Kylo's Clues

Knowing the meanings of common Latin and Greek roots, prefixes, and suffixes can help you determine what a word means.

LATIN:		GREEK:	
dict:	to say or tell	demo:	people
mis:	to send	gram:	written or drawn
spec:	to see, watch, or observe	graph:	to write
		holo:	whole
trans:	across	morph:	change form or shape
vert:	to turn	poly:	many
		tele:	distant

Match the words to their definitions by using the Latin and Greek roots, prefixes, and suffixes above.

dismiss
transgalactic
perspective
dictate
hologram
democracy
polymorphous
convert
telegraph

- a whole, three-dimensional image formed by light beams
- to say what must happen
- a system of government in which the people vote for leaders and laws
- crossing the galaxy
- to send away
- a point of view
- a system for sending messages long distances
- taking on many different forms
- to turn someone or something into someone or something else

You Complete Me

A **complete sentence** has a subject and verb, and expresses a complete thought. An **incomplete sentence** or **fragment** lacks a subject or verb, or does not express a complete thought.

Write a C next to the complete sentences. Write an I next to the incomplete sentences.

Anakin and Padmé married secretly. C

When they traveled together to Naboo. I

Because Jedi were not allowed to marry. I

R2-D2 and C-3PO were the only guests at the wedding. C

A spy told Emperor Palpatine about the wedding. C

To tempt Anakin toward the dark side. I

Rewrite the incomplete sentences so that they are complete.

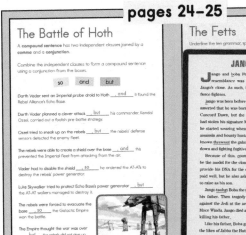

pages 24–25

The Battle of Hoth

A **compound sentence** has two independent clauses joined by a **comma** and a **conjunction**.

Combine the independent clauses to form a compound sentence using a conjunction from the boxes.

so · and · but

Darth Vader sent an Imperial probe droid to Hoth , and it found the Rebel Alliance's Echo Base.

Darth Vader planned a clever attack , but his commander, Kendal Ozzel, carried out a foolish pre-battle strategy.

Ozzel tried to sneak up on the rebels , but the rebels' defense sensors detected the enemy fleet.

The rebels were able to create a shield over the base , and this prevented the Imperial fleet from attacking from the air.

Vader had to disable the shield , so he ordered the AT-ATs to destroy the rebels' power generator.

Luke Skywalker tried to protect Echo Base's power generator , but the AT-AT walkers managed to destroy it.

The rebels were forced to evacuate the base , so the Galactic Empire won the battle.

The Empire thought the war was over , but the rebels did not give up.

The Fetts

Underline the ten grammar, spelling, and punctuation mistakes in this story.

JANGO AND BOBA

Jango and boba Fett were like father and son. The family resemblance was greater than usual, because Boba was Jango's clone. As such, both were expert trackers and fierce fighters.

jango was born before the Invasion of Naboo. Jango asserted that he was born on the Mandalorian planet Concord Dawn, but the Mandalorians claimed he had stolen his signature Mandalorian Armor, which he started wearing when he began working as an assassin and bounty hunter for hire. Jango became known threwout the galaxy for his skill in tracking down and fighting fugitives.

Because of this, count Dooku chose Jango to be the model for the clone soldiers he was creating. Fett agreed to provide his DNA for the clones and oversee their training. He was paid well, but he also asked for something else—one of the clones to raise as his son.

Jango taught Boba the mandalorian ways. Boba loved and revered his father. Then tragedy struck. Jango sided with Count Dooku against the Jedi at the arena in geonosis and was forced to battle Mace Windu. Jango died as Boba looked on. Boba hated the Jedi for killing his father.

Like his father, Boba grew up to be a bounty hunter, working for the likes of Jabba the Hutt and Darth Vader.

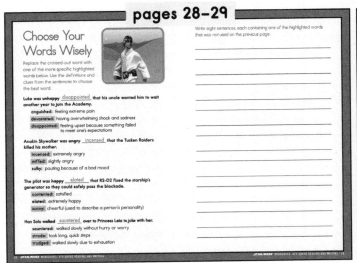

pages 26–27

Jar Jar Jumble

A **run-on sentence** is a series of two or more independent clauses that are not separated by a conjunction, semicolon, or period.

Incorrect:
Jar Jar Binks caused a flood at an important party he was banished from Otoh Gunga.

Correct:
Jar Jar Binks caused a flood at an important party, so he was banished from Otoh Gunga.

Rewrite the run-on sentences as compound sentences by adding commas and conjunctions from the boxes.

so · and · but

Qui-Gon, Obi-Wan, and Jar Jar traveled to Theed they rescued Queen Amidala there.
Qui-Gon, Obi-Wan, and Jar Jar traveled to Theed, and they rescued Queen Amidala there.

The four tried to fly to Coruscant their starship was damaged they landed on Tatooine.
The four tried to fly to Coruscant, but their starship was damaged, so they landed on Tatooine.

They needed to fix the starship Anakin said he could earn money by podracing.
They needed to fix the starship, so Anakin said he could earn money by podracing.

Anakin won the heroes left Tatooine.
Anakin won, and the heroes left Tatooine.

Queen Amidala pleaded her case to the Senate they would not help Naboo gain independence.
Queen Amidala pleaded her case to the Senate, but they would not help Naboo gain independence.

Queen Amidala joined forces with the Gungan Grand Army Jar Jar became Bombad General.
Queen Amidala joined forces with the Gungan Grand Army, and Jar Jar became Bombad General.

pages 28–29

Choose Your Words Wisely

Replace the crossed-out word with one of the more specific highlighted words below. Use the definitions and clues from the sentences to choose the best word.

Luke was unhappy disappointed that his uncle wanted him to wait another year to join the Academy.
- anguished: feeling extreme pain
- devastated: having overwhelming shock and sadness
- disappointed: feeling upset because something failed to meet one's expectations

Anakin Skywalker was angry incensed that the Tusken Raiders killed his mother.
- incensed: extremely angry
- miffed: slightly angry
- sulky: pouting because of a bad mood

The pilot was happy elated that R2-D2 fixed the starship's generator so they could safely pass the blockade.
- contented: satisfied
- elated: extremely happy
- sunny: cheerful (used to describe a person's personality)

Han Solo walked sauntered over to Princess Leia to joke with her.
- sauntered: walked slowly without hurry or worry
- strode: took long, quick steps
- trudged: walked slowly due to exhaustion

Write eight sentences, each containing one of the highlighted words that was not used on the previous page.

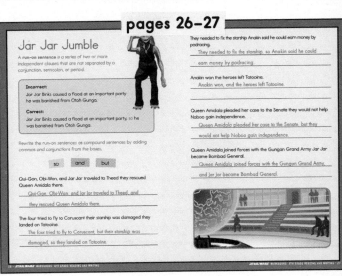

pages 30–31

Droid Disaster

Read the story of C-3PO's experience.

C-3PO just had a **harrid** adventure. It seems to happen to him a lot! This time, he was visited by his old friend Anakin Skywalker. As a boy, Anakin built C-3PO from spare parts. Anakin is still grown up now, however, and is a great Jedi instead of a slave. This made C-3PO swell with pride, until he realized that he may get swept up in Anakin's attempt to rescue Obi-Wan Kenobi.

To **accomplish** this dangerous mission, C-3PO and R2-D2 journeyed to the planet Geonosis with Anakin and Padmé. Once there, R2-D2 volunteered to help the humans. C-3PO worried that R2-D2 was too **obtuse** for this and had no sense of when he was needed or wanted. Well, R2-D2 didn't listen, and he followed Anakin and Padmé into the factory. C-3PO, a loyal friend, went too, only to be greeted by a distressing sight: droids making droids!

Before they knew it, R2-D2 **thrust** C-3PO onto the factory floor! That's when everything became **topsy-turvy**. C-3PO's head was attached to a battle droid's body! What a disaster! C-3PO was originally **programmed** to help, not hurt, so he was terribly embarrassed by his behavior on the battlefield. Attacking Jedi, name-calling, and firing a weapon—to what level would he stoop next?

All of a sudden, C-3PO's head went **soaring** off of his new body and onto the ground. Along came R2-D2, who dragged C-3PO's head over to his real body. C-3PO finally had a good head on his shoulders once again. In the end, R2-D2 was there to help his friend in trouble. Of course, R2-D2 was usually the one to start the trouble in the first place.

Context is the words or phrases that help define an unknown word's meaning. Context clues can appear within the same sentence as the unknown word, or they may be nearby in the passage.

"To accomplish this dangerous mission, C-3PO and R2-D2 journeyed to the planet . . ."

Based on the context in the story, what do you think the following words mean?

obtuse
- [ ] brave
- [ ] cautiously optimistic
- [x] slow to understand

programmed
- [ ] destroyed
- [x] designed
- [ ] brainwashed

soaring
- [ ] trickling
- [x] flying
- [ ] jumping

accomplish
- [x] complete
- [ ] complain
- [ ] ignore

thrust
- [x] pushed
- [ ] showed
- [ ] skipped

topsy-turvy
- [ ] exhilarating
- [x] upside-down or all mixed up
- [ ] swerving uncontrollably

horrid
- [x] terrifying
- [ ] quick
- [ ] exciting

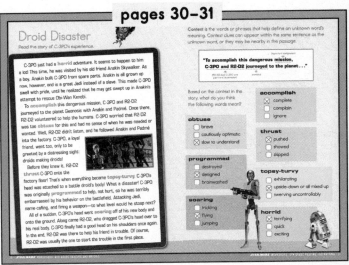

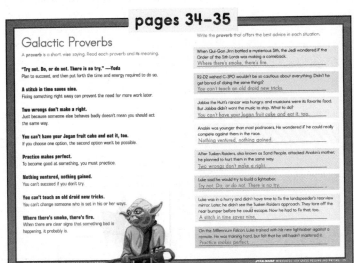

pages 34–35

Galactic Proverbs

A **proverb** is a short, wise saying. Read each proverb and its meaning.

"Try not. Do, or do not. There is no try." —Yoda
Plan to succeed, and then put forth the time and energy required to do so.

A stitch in time saves nine.
Fixing something right away can prevent the need for more work later.

Two wrongs don't make a right.
Just because someone else behaves badly doesn't mean you should act the same way.

You can't have your Jogan fruit cake and eat it, too.
If you choose one option, the second option won't be possible.

Practice makes perfect.
To become good at something, you must practice.

Nothing ventured, nothing gained.
You can't succeed if you don't try.

You can't teach an old droid new tricks.
You can't change someone who is set in his or her ways.

Where there's smoke, there's fire.
When there are clear signs that something bad is happening, it probably is.

Write the proverb that offers the best advice in each situation.

When Qui-Gon Jinn battled a mysterious Sith, the Jedi wondered if the Order of the Sith Lords was making a comeback.
Where there's smoke, there's fire.

R2-D2 wished C-3PO wouldn't be so cautious about everything. Didn't he get bored of doing the same things?
You can't teach an old droid new tricks.

Jabba the Hutt's rancor was hungry, and musicians were its favorite food. But Jabba didn't want the music to stop. What to do?
You can't have your Jogan fruit cake and eat it, too.

Anakin was younger than most podracers. He wondered if he could really compete against them in the race.
Nothing ventured, nothing gained.

After Tusken Raiders, also known as Sand People, attacked Anakin's mother, he planned to hurt them in the same way.
Two wrongs don't make a right.

Luke said he would try to build a lightsaber.
Try not. Do, or do not. There is no try.

Luke was in a hurry and didn't have time to fix the landspeeder's rearview mirror. Later, he didn't see the Tusken Raiders approach. They tore off the rear bumper before he could escape. Now he had to fix that, too.
A stitch in time saves nine.

On the Millennium Falcon, Luke trained with his new lightsaber against a remote. He was training hard, but felt that he still hadn't mastered it.
Practice makes perfect.

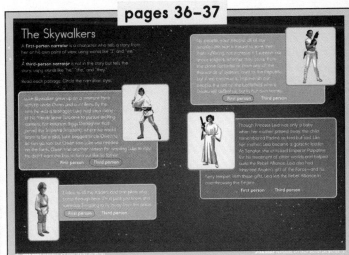

pages 36–37

The Skywalkers

A **first-person narrator** is a character who tells a story from her or his own point of view, using words like "I" and "we."

A **third-person narrator** is not in the story but tells the story, using words like "he," "she," and "they."

Read each passage. Circle the narration style.

First person · Third person

First person · Third person

First person · Third person

First person · Third person

Answers

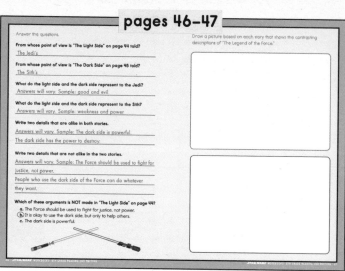

Answer the questions.

From whose point of view is "The Light Side" on page 44 told?
The Jedi's

From whose point of view is "The Dark Side" on page 45 told?
The Sith's

What do the light side and the dark side represent to the Jedi?
Answers will vary. Sample: good and evil

What do the light side and the dark side represent to the Sith?
Answers will vary. Sample: weakness and power

Write two details that are alike in both stories.
Answers will vary. Sample: The dark side is powerful.
The dark side has the power to destroy.

Write two details that are not alike in the two stories.
Answers will vary. Sample: The Force should be used to fight for
justice, not power.
People who use the dark side of the Force can do whatever
they want.

Which of these arguments is NOT made in "The Light Side" on page 44?
a. The Force should be used to fight for justice, not power.
b. It is okay to use the dark side, but only to help others.
c. The dark side is powerful.

Draw a picture based on each story that shows the contrasting
descriptions of "The Legend of the Force."

An Ode for Anakin

A **verse** in a poem is a group of lines. Verses are separated by a
blank line. **Rhyme scheme** is the way the words in a poem rhyme. Read
the following poem about Anakin aloud.

Anakin's Fall

He was the Chosen One.
The pride of Qui-Gon.
How did he fall so far
From where he had begun?

They meet again on Mustafar.
Padmé tells the truth; Anakin calls her a liar.
Qui-Gon must protect Padmé from his rage.
Anakin is on the dark side of this war.

They fight beside the angry sea.
Who will be the one to go free?

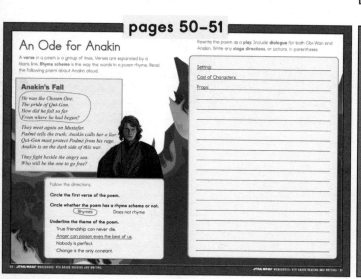

Follow the directions.

Circle the first verse of the poem.

Circle whether the poem has a rhyme scheme or not.
Rhymes   Does not rhyme

Underline the theme of the poem.
True friendship can never die.
Anger can poison even the best of us.
Nobody is perfect.
Change is the only constant.

Rewrite the poem as a **play**. Include **dialogue** for both Obi-Wan and
Anakin. Write any **stage directions**, or actions, in parentheses.

Setting:
Cast of Characters:
Props:

A **main idea** tells what a story is about. **Supporting details** are facts,
descriptions, and examples that help prove or illustrate the main idea.

Follow the directions.

Circle the main idea of this text.
Even though the clone troopers were similar to one another, the Jedi saw
each as an individual.
Clone troopers were brave and capable, but also dangerous because they
followed orders without question.
Palpatine betrayed the Empire when he ordered the Jedi to be killed.

**Circle the supporting detail from the text that suggests that the Sith
were behind the creation of the clone troopers all along.**
The Kaminoans had been waiting for a Jedi to arrive to claim the army.
Led by their Jedi generals, the clones fought the Separatist army bravely.
Sifo-Dyas was killed by a Sith, who took over the operation of creating
the clone army.

**Why was it so dangerous for the clone troopers not to be able to think for
themselves? Support your argument with details and examples from the text.**
Answers will vary. Sample: They would follow orders—even bad
ones—without question. The danger of this was shown when they
were ordered to kill the Jedi, and they did it without stopping to
think that it was wrong.

**Why was Jango Fett used as a model for clone troopers? Support your
argument with details and examples from the text.**
Answers will vary. Sample: As a bounty hunter, Jango Fett had discipline, concentration, and athleticism—all good qualities for a soldier.

**If you were a Jedi who trained the clone troopers, what types of
orders would you tell them to follow or not follow?**
You should follow orders that
You shouldn't follow orders that

A **firsthand account** is based on the author's personal experience.
Examples include a diary, autobiography, or personal blog post.
A **secondhand account** is based on the author's research. It may
include information from an article or history book.

Pretend you are a clone trooper. Write a firsthand account about
your training as a soldier.

As a clone trooper, I

Compare your firsthand account with the
secondhand account on pages 52–53.

**What does your firsthand account have that the
secondhand account does not?**

**What does the secondhand account have that your
firsthand account does not?**

Worlds Apart

Read about the home planets.

Father and son, Anakin and Luke Skywalker were both raised on the desert
planet Tatooine. With two suns, it was quite hot during the day. It was so remote
that neither the Galactic Republic nor the Empire considered it to be under their
domain. Instead, the Hutts—a crime family—ruled the planet. In spite of its remote
location, it did have a few port cities, including Mos Espa, where Anakin and his
mother, Shmi, were slaves to a junk dealer.

Had Anakin not fallen to the dark side, Luke and Leia likely would have been
raised on Coruscant, where their mother served in the Senate and their father
served on the Jedi Council. Instead, Leia was adopted by Bail Organa and Queen
Breha of Alderaan, and Luke was taken as a baby to live on Tatooine. Though this
planet was no less dry or remote than it had been when Anakin was a boy, Luke did
enjoy a more comfortable childhood. His aunt and uncle were moisture farmers,
using technology to collect water vapor from the air. Though it wasn't a luxurious
lifestyle, Luke's family owned a relatively large house, land, and several droids who
aided them in their work.

Mother and daughter, Padmé Amidala and Leia Organa grew up on different
planets—both green and lush. Naboo and Alderaan were similar in each other
and very different from Tatooine. Padmé's native Naboo had a watery core where
Gungans lived in bubble cities. The surface of the planet was also rich in water.
The capital city of Theed was built alongside a river, and beautiful waterfalls
cascaded down from the royal palaces, where Padmé served as queen. Naboo and
Alderaan both had picturesque countrysides where people farmed. Their cities
were rich in culture and wisdom and were home to more than a few universities.
They were the kind of planets you would never want to leave. However, Padmé
and Leia were not content to enjoy the comforts of home. Instead, they became
inspiring leaders and traveled far and wide to promote peace and justice.

Circle the correct answer to each question.

How is this text organized?
To show events in chronological order   To compare and contrast things

Which of the following is true, according to the text?
Tatooine, Naboo, and Alderaan are all very different from one another.
Tatooine and Naboo are similar, but Alderaan is different from both.
Tatooine is different from both Naboo and Alderaan, which are similar to each other.

Best Base Planet

An **opinion piece** is a text that expresses your beliefs about a topic.
Pretend you are a leader in the Rebel Alliance. Write an opinion piece
to your crew about why you believe the fleet must go to Tatooine,
Naboo, or Alderaan. To support your opinion, include information about
the landscape, weather, and opportunities to find new military bases.

Answer the questions about the timeline on pages 78–79.

**Name two other things that happen the year that Luke and Leia
are born.**
Answers will vary. Sample: Anakin becomes Darth Vader.
Anakin is badly burned while fighting Obi-Wan Kenobi on
Mustafar.

Number these events in the correct order:
The first Death Star is destroyed.   3
Anakin Skywalker becomes a Sith.   1
Emperor Palpatine dies.   4
Princess Leia grows up on Alderaan.   2

Which year came first, 19 BBY or 46 BBY?
46 BBY

Which year came first, 3 ABY or 4 ABY?
3 ABY

How old were Leia and Luke during the Battle of Yavin?
19

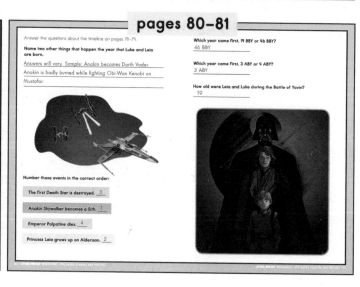